# SOUTHERN BULLDOG NORTHERN BULLDOG

The Georgia-Yale Series of 1923-34

Douglas S. Malan

Published by Alzancas Press

November 2018

# SOUTHERN BULLDOG, NORTHERN BULLDOG
The Georgia-Yale Series of 1923-34

Copyright © 2018 by Douglas S. Malan

All rights reserved. No part of this book may be used or reproduced by any means, graphic, electronic, or mechanical, including photocopying, recording, taping or by any information storage retrieval system without the written permission of the author and publisher except in the case of brief quotations embodied in articles and reviews.

Alzancas Press
Maple Hill, Connecticut
www.douglasmalan.com

Because of the dynamic nature of the internet, any web addresses or links contained in this book may have changed since publication and may no longer be valid.

The views expressed in this work are solely those of the author and do not necessarily reflect the views of the publisher, and the publisher hereby disclaims any responsibility for them.

ISBN: 9781734713701 (pbk)
ISBN: 9781734713718 (ebk)

Printed in the United States of America

I dedicate this work to Allison, Alexander and Lucas. Thank you for always encouraging me to spend more time on my creative projects and supporting me along the various paths I travel.

# TABLE OF CONTENTS

Preface . . . . . . . . . . . . . . . . . . . . . . . . . . . . . . . . . . . 7
Introduction . . . . . . . . . . . . . . . . . . . . . . . . . . . . . . . 13
October 13, 1923 . . . . . . . . . . . . . . . . . . . . . . . . . . . . 25
October 11, 1924 . . . . . . . . . . . . . . . . . . . . . . . . . . . . 37
October 10, 1925 . . . . . . . . . . . . . . . . . . . . . . . . . . . . 47
October 9, 1926 . . . . . . . . . . . . . . . . . . . . . . . . . . . . . 57
October 8, 1927 . . . . . . . . . . . . . . . . . . . . . . . . . . . . . 67
October 13, 1928 . . . . . . . . . . . . . . . . . . . . . . . . . . . . 81
The Invitation . . . . . . . . . . . . . . . . . . . . . . . . . . . . . . 89
October 12, 1929 . . . . . . . . . . . . . . . . . . . . . . . . . . . . 95
October 11, 1930 . . . . . . . . . . . . . . . . . . . . . . . . . . . . 117
October 10, 1931 . . . . . . . . . . . . . . . . . . . . . . . . . . . . 127
1932 . . . . . . . . . . . . . . . . . . . . . . . . . . . . . . . . . . . . . 137
November 11, 1933 . . . . . . . . . . . . . . . . . . . . . . . . . . 139
November 10, 1934 . . . . . . . . . . . . . . . . . . . . . . . . . . 149
Epilogue . . . . . . . . . . . . . . . . . . . . . . . . . . . . . . . . . 159
Selected References . . . . . . . . . . . . . . . . . . . . . . . . . 165

# PREFACE

My uncle, Dr. Clarence Eugene Cawvey, earned his undergraduate degree from Yale in 1951. Because of him, the Yale Bulldogs were one of the first sports teams I knew. Uncle Gene, a general physician in our then-booming coal town, lived down the street from us in a secluded Victorian manor house surrounded by wild tangles of trees and bushes on the manicured property's periphery.

Growing up, I remember hearing stories about the trolley traffic leading to Yale Bowl on game days and the world-class pizzas served on Wooster Street. I believe Yale played the only football games my uncle would watch, and I know Wooster Street was the only place he would eat pizza in the United States. Living in our small town of Pinckneyville, Illinois, my uncle deprived himself of football and pizza for most of his life.

After one of Uncle Gene's trips to New Haven for a class reunion, he brought back a small white sweatshirt. The

## Southern Bulldog, Northern Bulldog

imprint was raised and rubbery. Handsome Dan smoked his pipe and leaned on a sturdy blue "Y" outlined in white, part of "YALE" printed in bold simplicity. I already sensed something regal in the name, a certain power in the single syllable, even though I knew little about the university other than its location in the exotic region of New England. That sweatshirt became special, not something I'd throw on to play football in the yard. Most of the time, it hung in my closet and I'd study the logo and feel the textured material. I wore the sweatshirt only if I knew I wouldn't stain it. Even when I outgrew the shirt, I kept it.

Yale football always represented something rugged and scholarly to me, the archetype of a student-athlete Walter Camp helped create as he was shaping the game. Yale was debonair, heroic, historic, nail-tough and tack-sharp. All I had as reference was my uncle, and he seemed to be most of these.

From my parents, I received an introduction to Georgia football from stories they told about their days living in Columbus, and I heard plenty about Alabama football, too. To a young boy in the Midwest, those schools sounded exciting and different. In the days before broadcast saturation, I watched only the Big 10 and Grambling State University, because ESPN covered Eddie Robinson's chase of Bear Bryant for all-time coaching wins. Georgia. Alabama. Tennessee. Auburn. Bowl games brought those schools into my home during Christmas vacation and they were more fascinating than many NFL teams.

My path took me south where I learned the truth behind the words of former Alcorn State and Southern University

# Preface

Head Coach Marino Casem: "In the South, football is a religion, and Saturday is the holy day." Growing up in Big 10 country exposed me to rich traditions and power football. In the South, I experienced pageantry and passion beyond anything I had seen. College football in the South is a different language, spoken in fiery native tongues during massive block parties attracting tens of thousands of people every Saturday. It's not at all genteel like other elements of Southern front-porch culture, and certainly not as reserved as the New England crowd at Yale Bowl.

Morgan Blake's report from the 1916 Georgia-Georgia Tech game in the Atlanta Constitution captures the spirit often found today at southern games. "Even those who had imbibed pretty freely... maintained splendid decorum. There were very few hoodlum drunks. Of those who were intoxicated, most of them were drunk in a dignified sense."

I am fortunate to have experienced the spectacle of college football as different regions of the country interpret it. There was a time in college football history when these intersectional clashes were rare and the various types of

*Fay Vincent was a three-year starter on Yale's football team from 1928 to 1930.*

celebrations largely unknown. Georgia-Yale played out during such a time.

The catalyst for this project was Francis "Fay" T. Vincent, Jr., to whom I am grateful for his generosity and for introducing me to the Yale-Georgia story. While working on a separate book, I contacted Mr. Vincent and shared a photo of his father, an accomplished football and baseball player at Yale, I found during my research. Mr. Vincent invited me to his home to look through his father's scrapbook of baseball and football clippings. During that visit, I discovered the Yale players' itinerary card for the Bulldogs' historic trip to Athens, Georgia, in 1929. The artifact and our conversation around it sparked my interest in this fascinating link between Yale and Georgia, and I was inspired to chronicle this brief series as a nod to my upbringing and appreciation of history.

# Preface

# INTRODUCTION

The 900 miles separating New Haven, Connecticut, and Athens, Georgia, seem, at first glance, to be as common as the distance between Baton Rouge and Iowa City or Tuscaloosa and State College.

College football teams in those towns are powerful and connected to each other through a discussion of signature programs playing in elite conferences. What differentiates the New Haven and Athens connection, though, is a kinship between the flagship universities in these cities that reduces those 900 miles to something more intimate and tangible, a familial connection as old as the University of Georgia and Athens themselves. Sister-city relationships are common between far-flung locales that share all manner of similarities in culture, spirit or otherwise. New Haven and Athens go deeper.

This story of the unique Yale-Georgia rivalry from the 1920s and 1930s is much older than it seems. Considering 86 years have passed since they last played football and their programs now exist in different worlds, this rivalry already was an interesting footnote of early 20th century college football history far removed from the collective consciousness. But if not for a bond formed several centuries ago, one that today's students may know little of, the football rivalry would never exist.

It all started with Lyman Hall, a Yale graduate, physician, clergyman and statesmen – a signer of the Declaration of Independence. He migrated south from Connecticut in the mid-1700s and eventually settled in Georgia where he was elected governor of America's thirteenth colony.

With his plan to create an educational system in Georgia, Hall recruited Abraham Baldwin – also a Yale graduate, minister and politician – to move to Georgia where he became a successful lawyer and politician, serving as one of Georgia's two signatories to the U.S. Constitution. Hall, likely with Baldwin's assistance, convinced the Georgia Legislature to grant 40,000 acres of land for a college in 1784, and Baldwin drafted the charter for the first land-grant university in America. In 1785, Hall appointed Baldwin as the first president of the University of Georgia. Tracts of land were sold in ensuing years to raise money for the university's physical structures and those acres sprouted the city of Athens while the old campus was situated on approximately 40 acres remaining of the original 40,000.

Yale's influence on the University of Georgia was prevalent, beyond the men who formed the university. Georgia's curriculum mirrored Yale's classical courses that emphasized Latin and Greek while growing to include science and mathematics. One of the first buildings constructed on North

## Introduction

Campus, the Franklin College of Arts and Sciences, now known as Old College, was modeled architecturally after Connecticut Hall on Yale's campus. As Georgia prepared to open its doors to its first class of students in 1801, Baldwin stepped aside for Josiah Meigs, yet another Yale graduate and a former lawyer in Connecticut, to serve as president.

And more than a century later, following a brief period of using a goat as a mascot, Georgia athletics chose an English Bulldog to represent its teams, though Yale had no influence on that decision.

Yale already was considered college football royalty by the 1870s after adopting the game from New Jersey and becoming an Eastern powerhouse with Princeton and Harvard. Bulldog player/coach/advocate Walter Camp was busy earning his sobriquet "The Father of American Football" as he transformed the sport from brutish street fight with 20 men per side into the more structured game we know today, all while holding his day job at the New Haven Clock Company.

The Bulldogs had won more than half of their 27 national championships by the time football arrived at the University of Georgia. The catalyst in Athens was chemistry professor Dr. Charles Herty, who earned his PhD at Johns Hopkins University and studied a good bit of football in the process. Herty, known for revolutionizing the turpentine industry in America, organized Georgia's first varsity team to meet Mercer on January 30, 1892, in an open field on campus that is now a plaza with a cascading fountain. Georgia won that inaugural game, 50-0, creating an unprecedented buzz in Athens for college football.

## Southern Bulldog, Northern Bulldog

Herty wanted to capitalize on the excitement and he contacted Dr. George Petrie, his football-loving classmate at Johns Hopkins who was at Auburn University. Petrie formed Auburn's first varsity football team and coached them to a 10-0 win over Herty and Georgia later in 1892, the first game in the Deep South's Oldest Rivalry. Because of their mutual interest in bringing football to their campuses, Herty and Petrie soon became the first athletic directors at their universities.

Games against Georgia Tech were scheduled, and Georgia grew increasingly serious about its football. In 1895, the university gave Glenn "Pop" Warner one of his first head coaching jobs, paying the former Cornell star $34 a week to lure him away from Iowa State, and his battles against Auburn and head coach John Heisman became legendary. In November 1895, there was talk of Yale and Georgia meeting on the gridiron – in Athens, no less – but the proposed deal was unsanctioned, the result of New Haven attorney George B. Hall talking to Yale players about getting together a game in Georgia to make money on the side. The start of the rivalry would wait nearly 30 years; meanwhile, the Southern Bulldogs continued to evolve into a regional gridiron force.

Georgia logged a perfect season in 1896, capped by a win over Auburn in front of 8,000 people at Brisbane Park in Atlanta, the largest crowd to see a college football game south of Philadelphia. In response, Herty launched into what is now an age-old practice – hitting up alumni for more money to support a successful program. Georgia had "come to the top with the poorest equipment in the South," Herty told the Atlanta newspaper, and he eventually raised $1,900 to improve "our old red dirt field" in Athens.

# Introduction

All that momentum was stopped cold by tragedy in 1897 when Georgia fullback Von Gammon died from severe head injuries suffered in a game against the University of Virginia. Football immediately ceased at Georgia, Georgia Tech and Mercer. The state's General Assembly pushed through a bill outlawing football in all schools receiving state funds, and it needed only Governor William Yates Atkinson's signature to become law.

Von Gammon's mother, Rosalind Burns Gammon, was grieving her son's death, but knew how much football meant to him.

"Grant me the right to request that my boy's death should not be used to defeat the most cherished object of his life," she wrote in an emotional plea that reached Atkinson, just in time for him to veto the bill.

Violence in football remained a significant problem, one that Walter Camp knew well as the head of a committee charged with investigating and researching the frequency of injuries and death. At President Teddy Roosevelt's behest, Camp and other distinguished members of the university community formed the Intercollegiate Football Rules Committee (IFRC) in 1905, a forerunner to the National Collegiate Athletic Association (NCAA) of today.

Stricter rules were enacted to clean up the game and create many of the basic elements we know today, such as 11 men per side, four downs to gain 10 yards, and the forward pass. The changes were designed to eliminate the use of dangerous plays like the flying wedge, powered by large clusters of men slamming into each other at full speed. Even the scoring structure was evolving into something familiar – conversions after touchdowns scored one point and safeties scored two in 1906 while field goals dropped from five points to three in 1910 and touchdowns increased from five points to six in 1912.

With football reinstated at Georgia after the Von Gammon tragedy, Steadman Vincent Sanford, an English literature professor at the university when he arrived in 1903, became the driving force behind Georgia's ascension in the college football world. While he was founding the school's journalism department and later serving as the dean, Sanford envisioned a brighter future for the university, and it would grow from the marshy bottomland between the campuses of Franklin College and the Agricultural College.

In "The Ghosts of Herty Field," published in 1966, John F. Stegeman set the scene:

*Sanford Stadium, as depicted on a postcard from the 1940s.*

## Introduction

*"Near the Central of Georgia railroad tracks the area was so inaccessible that the rifle team practiced there without fear of hitting anyone with stray bullets. Otherwise only an occasional nature-lover strolled through the lonely glen, as did Professor Sanford, who was interested not so much in the beauty of the scene as with a vision that was haunting him: a natural bowl with a football fleld in the hollow. The reverie of this kindly English teacher and the administrative energy of the same man years later were largely responsible for the transformation of that damp and shadowy valley into the beautiful Sanford Stadium of today."*

There were a few Southern schools ahead of Georgia's curve – namely Vanderbilt University, the University of Virginia and the University of North Carolina. All three started their football programs between 1888 and 1890, and all three represented the Southern football aristocracy when they became the region's first to play intersectional games in the East against Harvard, Yale and the University of Pennsylvania in the 1900s and 1910s.

During this time, the farthest north Georgia played was Annapolis, Maryland, site of a 27-3 loss to Navy in October 1916. But the Southern Bulldogs gained more national exposure with the hiring of head coach Herman J. Stegeman, who had played for Amos Alonzo Stagg (former Yale All-American) at the University of Chicago. Stegeman's first Georgia team in 1920 fashioned an 8-0-1 record and captured the Southern Conference championship.

Opportunities to play traditional powers in the East and North soon presented themselves to Stegeman and his Bulldogs. In 1921, Georgia traveled north of the Mason-Dixon Line for the first time, taking on powerhouse Harvard in Cambridge, Massachusetts. No team had scored on Harvard in six games dating to the 1920 season and the Crimson were riding a 23-game unbeaten streak when Georgia rolled into the Boston area. Experts figured they had no chance, but the Bulldogs pinned Harvard to the ropes for a time before losing a hard-fought 10-7 decision.

Stories of Georgia's valiant efforts spread quickly through the South. Scoring updates were announced during Georgia Tech's game and those fans who normally hated Georgia cheered the Southern Bulldogs each time. It was a statement game for Georgia and other Southern schools. (Interestingly, two weeks after Georgia nearly upset Harvard, tiny Centre College of Danville, Kentucky, shocked the Crimson in one of the greatest upsets in college football history.)

At the end of the 1921 season, Georgia hosted another Eastern power, Dartmouth, which traveled from New Hampshire to Atlanta to capture a 7-0 victory. In 1922, the Bulldogs paid a visit to Stegeman's alma mater in Chicago, Georgia's first trip to the Midwest, and dropped a 20-0 contest. Three games against programs with national appeal resulted in three losses. But Georgia was increasing its exposure in other parts of the country, and this continued with the Yale series, which began in 1923.

Yale football was entrenched in the national psyche. Walter Camp had been writing prolifically through the years about college football, creating a mystique around the scholarly Yale man who proudly represents his school in Saturday battles on the gridiron. Yale football was so big that Camp came up with the idea to use a powerful football program to

## Introduction

provide funding for minor sports, or what we call non-revenue sports today.

Yale played football as an independent, the Ivy League not being formed officially until 1954, and called its own shots. If you wanted to play Yale, you came to New Haven. After all, Yale Bowl was there, the largest stadium in the world and the first to use a bowl design when it opened for the Harvard game in 1914. Yale Bowl rivaled Rome's Colosseum in awe-inspiring design, for which Thomas C. Atwood, an MIT man, was responsible as chief engineer on the project.

When it hosted its first game in 1914, Yale Bowl was the largest stadium in the world, with seating for 70,000 fans, and the first to leverage a bowl design. Many other football stadia were inspired by Yale Bowl's design, including the Rose Bowl in Pasadena, California, and Georgia's Sanford Stadium.

Everything about Yale and the Bowl was magnificent and magnified. So, imagine a group of Georgia men making that train trip to New Haven in 1923, some leaving the Georgia countryside for the first time, to battle the mighty Northern Bulldogs of the world-class institution whose graduates were responsible for creating the University of Georgia and the charming city of Athens.

Such is how this rivalry started.

***Author's note:*** *In compiling the starting lineups and substitutes for each game, I relied on reports from the New York Times, Atlanta Constitution, Associated Press and United Press International. In some cases, there were discrepancies in positions played. In other cases, names were misspelled. I cross-checked all names with both schools' official lists of football lettermen; occasionally, newspapers printed surnames not found on the lettermen rosters, and I included those names to recognize the men who contributed to this unique rivalry.*

Introduction

George "Kid" Woodruff, right, served as Georgia's head coach from 1923, when the Yale series began, until 1927. He hired Harry Mehre, left, and Frank Thomas, center, as assistant coaches and introduced the Notre Dame offense to the South. The trio is seen in front of Sanford Stadium in 1930. Mehre went on to become head coach of Georgia and the University of Mississippi while Thomas became a highly successful head coach at the University of Alabama.

### OCTOBER 13, 1923

# YALE 40
# GEORGIA 0

### YALE BOWL
New Haven, Connecticut
Attendance 25,000

This familial intersectional rivalry commenced with a bold statement defining where each program stood in 1923. Yale was a college football blueblood going back to the origins of the game. Its former head coach, Walter Camp, codified the basic elements of the game we know today and helped create the mystique and spectacle of college football. Georgia, meanwhile, was one of the Deep South's first football programs, created in 1892 by a fine academic institution with cachet that attracted notable educators who were interested in growing the sport.

## Southern Bulldog, Northern Bulldog

Thomas Albert Dwight (T.A.D.) Jones, in his sixth season, served as Yale's head coach after a decorated career as Yale player, the path traveled by many Yale football coaches. Jones was an All-American quarterback in 1907 and integral part of dominant national championship teams in the mid-1900s. As head coach, he employed the single-wing attack, an offense created by former Georgia head coach Glenn "Pop" Warner that served as a precursor to the modern spread offense, and used it to steamroll North Carolina, 53-0, the week prior to hosting Georgia.

Georgia's head coach was first-year leader George Cecil "Kid" Woodruff, a captain of the 1911 Georgia team. Woodruff brought Knute Rockne's Notre Dame Box offense to the South and hired line coach Harry Mehre and backfield coach Frank Thomas, two of Rockne's former players, to teach the scheme. Thomas later became a coaching legend at Alabama while Mehre was being groomed to replace Woodruff later in the 1920s. Behind the Notre Dame shift attack, Georgia enjoyed a strong start to the 1923 season, knocking out Mercer and Oglethorpe by a combined 27-6 before traveling to New Haven.

The discrepancy between the coaches' salaries is interesting to note. As Yale's head coach, Jones earned $15,000 a year while Woodruff took a coaching salary of $1 per year due to his successful insurance business in Columbus, Georgia.

Although Georgia started its season with two wins, they paid a price. A handful of starters were knocked out with injuries, including John Fletcher, speedy halfback and All-Southern honoree in 1922. Their absences likely didn't affect the outcome of the Yale game, though.

October 13, 1923

Century Milstead, third from left, was a consensus All-American tackle in 1923, his only season with Yale. He poses here with fellow members of the 1930 Yale coaching staff, from left: Ducky Pond, Waldo Greene, Head Coach Mal Stevens, trainer George Connors, Adam Walsh, Charles Comerford and Richard Luman.

The Northern Bulldogs came out with a vengeance, proving to be as powerful as advertised while standing as one of Yale's greatest teams in the making. After the first quarter, Yale led 23-0, which played into projections that the stage was too big for the Southern Bulldogs. The Atlanta Constitution said as much in its wrap-up, noting the grandeur of Yale Bowl and Yale's mystique. In his syndicated newspaper column on

## Southern Bulldog, Northern Bulldog

September 24, Walter Camp had also predicted stage fright for Georgia in its first trip to New Haven.

Yale, however, was a tremendous force and certainly didn't prevail solely because of its visitors' anxiety, if any existed. The Bulldogs' passing game behind Mal Stevens, a Yale medical student who came from Washburn University in Kansas and played only the 1923 season for the Elis, was on point when called upon, and the running game, anchored by All-American tackle and future New York Giant Century Milstead, consistently sliced through Georgia's defense.

Three minutes into the game, Yale struck when Milstead, a one-year Yale man who transferred from Wabash College in Indiana, blocked a punt by Georgia captain Joe Bennett after a low snap and recovered on the 5-yard line. Yale's Raymond Pond went to work smashing into Georgia's line for a couple of yards before Stevens plunged into the end zone on a short burst. Stevens added the drop-kick extra point for a 7-0 Yale lead.

Georgia got the ball back deep in its own territory, choosing to punt away from the 9-yard line. Stevens fielded Bennett's kick around the 50 and scampered through Georgia's coverage down to the Southern Bulldogs' 12. Stevens picked up five yards on the first play, Pond tore through for four on the next and then capped it with a touchdown run from three yards out. Stevens lined up the extra-point kick, but Bennett blasted through the wall to block the attempt. Yale led 13-0 after only a handful of plays on offense.

When Yale got the ball back, Stevens immediately punted after a 32-yard return by Russell Murphy to pin Georgia

October 13, 1923

deep in its own territory. The strategy worked. Martin Kilpatrick fielded the punt for Georgia and promptly fumbled at the 14-yard line where opportunistic Yale center Winslow Lovejoy waited to recover.

The Southern Bulldogs held their ground for three downs, but Stevens chalked up points with a drop-kick field goal on fourth down and a 16-0 lead after fewer than 10 minutes had run off the game clock. Yale's onslaught continued.

Stevens, Yale's do-it-all halfback, inspired the Northern Bulldogs on their next drive from midfield with a 30-yard pass to Russell Murphy on first down. Captain and fullback "Memphis Bill" Mallory ripped off a 15-yard run around left end and Stevens burst up the middle for a five-yard touchdown while adding the extra point.

After falling behind quickly, some observers expected Georgia to regain its footing as it had in the Harvard game of 1921 when the Southern Bulldogs gamely battled the mighty Crimson. Indeed, Georgia fought back, but was unable to overcome Yale's quick start and relentless pressure.

Joe Bennett blocked a punt for Georgia to set up the Bulldogs in prime position at Yale's 13-yard line, and the Yale faithful were pulling for the Southerners to put points on the board. But Yale's defense stuffed Georgia and forced Bennett to attempt a field goal, which he missed as the first quarter ended with Yale in command, 23-0.

Georgia took some momentum into its second-quarter drives and picked up several first downs. Again, the Northern Bulldogs held when necessary and forced punts. While most of the second quarter was spent in Yale territory, the teams traded possessions and neither scored during the 15 minutes.

By halftime, the outcome was inevitable. Yale continued to drive on Georgia in the third quarter. Stevens capped the first drive with an impressive 30-yard field goal after Georgia's defense held, and then Pond scored from six yards out after a lengthy march, followed by a Stevens kick.

In the fourth quarter, Yale's final score was set up by a 15-yard Georgia penalty that placed the ball at the Southern Bulldogs' 15. Yale ran a fake pass play that turned into a powerful run through the center of the line by Hoxie Haas, captain of Yale's 1923 basketball team. Haas quickly covered 15 yards to the end zone and added the kick for the final spread.

Halfback Mal Stevens of Yale accounted for 21 points with two touchdowns, three extra-point kicks and two field goals. Pond also added two touchdowns and Haas contributed significantly in the series' largest margin of victory.

Yale ran for 110 yards on the afternoon and surrendered 97 yards to Georgia. The Elis were more proficient through the air with Stevens, who completed all six attempts for 74 yards to keep drives alive and set up pounding touchdown runs paved by Yale's overpowering line. Yale also established good field position by consistently breaking through Georgia's wall on numerous punt returns and taking advantage of fumbles.

Mallory, Yale's captain, carried the ball only twice. As the New York Times noted, Mallory's contributions came from his capabilities as a field general who could read Georgia's

October 13, 1923

maneuvers accurately and know where the Elis should strike. Fitting, because Memphis Bill later became a World War II Air Force intelligence officer and hero for cutting off Germany's supply lines into Italy during Operation Mallory.

Georgia, meanwhile, was limited to 2-of-12 passing, and the Southern Bulldogs were stymied each time they attempted the pass play that had worked so well against Harvard two seasons prior.

Bennett, the team captain and tackle, was Georgia's lone bright spot, described by the Atlanta newspaper as "more than half of the Georgia team" on this day with his two blocked kicks, sideline-to-sideline tackling and notable punting skills.

The series' inaugural game was a one-sided affair, but plenty of intrigue awaited fans, players and coaches.

Southern Bulldog, Northern Bulldog

# YALE

### STARTING LINEUP

| | |
|---|---|
| Head Coach: | Thomas Albert Dwight (T.A.D.) Jones |
| Ends: | Anton Hulman, Jr. and Richard Luman |
| Tackles: | Century Milstead and John Miller |
| Guards: | John Diller and Richard Eckhart |
| Center: | Winslow Lovejoy |
| Quarterback: | Russell Murphy |
| Halfbacks: | Marvin Stevens and Raymond Pond |
| Fullback: | William Mallory (Captain) |

### SUBSTITUTES

| | |
|---|---|
| End: | John Bingham |
| Tackle: | Edwin Blair |
| End: | John Lincoln, Jr. |
| Halfback: | Edward Bench |
| Center: | Houston Landis, Jr. |
| Halfback: | Edmund Cottle, Jr. |
| Halfback: | J. Hoxie Haas |
| Quarterback: | William Riley |
| Tackle: | Benjamin Butterworth |
| Center: | David Burt, Jr. |
| Tackle: | Edward Greene, Jr. |

October 13, 1923

# GEORGIA

### STARTING LINEUP

| | |
|---|---|
| Head Coach: | George "Kid" Woodruff |
| Ends: | Sam Richardson and James Thomason |
| Tackle: | N. James Taylor and Joe Bennett, Jr. (Captain) |
| Guards: | Ike Joselove and Spencer Grayson |
| Center: | T. Roosevelt Day |
| Quarterback: | Andrew Moore, Jr. |
| Halfbacks: | Martin Kilpatrick and Windham |
| Fullback: | Jacob Butler |

### SUBSTITUTES

| | |
|---|---|
| Center: | W. Maxwell Oliver, Jr. |
| Quarterback: | Charles Wiehrs |
| Halfback: | William Philpot |
| Halfback: | Tom Nelson |
| Guard: | Marshall Levie |
| Guard: | Wesley Bass |
| Halfback: | Slomwitz |
| Guard: | Tippin |

## Southern Bulldog, Northern Bulldog

After defeating Georgia, the Elis handled Army easily, shut out Princeton and Harvard, and capped a magnificent undefeated season with eight wins. The only scare was a come-from-behind 16-14 win over Maryland on November 10. In the 1923 version of The Game, T.A.D. Jones famously told his team, "Gentlemen, you are now going to play football against Harvard. Never again in your whole life will you do anything so important." In that battle, Pond earned his enduring sobriquet "Ducky" from iconic sportswriter Grantland Rice after scoring a long touchdown on a water-logged field in Cambridge. College football researchers retroactively named Yale 1923 national champions with Illinois and Michigan, and historians believe the '23 Bulldogs were the greatest of all Yale teams as they outscored their opponents 230-38. Regarding individual honors, Milstead and Mallory earned consensus All-American recognition.

The Southern Bulldogs recovered quickly from the loss in New Haven, shutting out Tennessee, Auburn and Virginia in succession. Then, they fizzled. Blowout losses at Vanderbilt and Alabama (combined 71-7) preceded a 3-3 decision at home against the mighty-mite Praying Colonels of Centre College. Georgia finished 5-3-1 in the middle of the 20-team Southern Conference.

October 13, 1923

*Yale captain and fullback "Memphis Bill" Mallory was a vital part of Yale's 1923 national championship team that dominated Georgia in the first game of the series. Mallory became a World War II hero and was inducted into the College Football Hall of Fame.*

## OCTOBER 11, 1924
# YALE 7
# GEORGIA 6

**YALE BOWL**
New Haven, Connecticut
Attendance 30,000

Yale came off its national championship season in search of backfield replacements after graduating Mallory and Stevens, but returning talent on the line kept expectations high for the Elis. Georgia, meanwhile, was looking for redemption after the humbling loss in 1923 that left their ears ringing.

Both teams cleaned up opponents easily before meeting in New Haven. Yale conquered North Carolina (27-0) while Georgia knocked off Mercer (26-7) and South Carolina

## Southern Bulldog, Northern Bulldog

(18-0) with impressive defensive performances that proved to be the hallmark of its 1924 team. As Woodruff devised his game plan for Yale, he did so without team captain and end John Fletcher, whose nagging early-season injuries kept him on the bench.

When the Bulldogs met each other in early October, the dramatic battle of defense and field position quickly took shape.

Georgia threw the first punch in this slugfest with its opportunistic defense. Yale took the opening kickoff and steadily drove into and through the Southern Bulldogs' wall with a series of run plays. Dan Allen, Yale's fullback, cracked the defense open with a long run around end down to Georgia's 20-yard line. But in tackling Allen, Georgia's defense stripped the ball and the Southern Bulldogs recovered to thwart the drive.

Georgia turned the tables with its own steady march on a succession of end runs, with halfback Charles Wiehrs leading the attack. A 12-yard run around right end, another 12 yards around left. A smash up the middle. When Wiehrs wasn't shouldering the load, halfback Tom Nelson was slamming his way through Yale defenders, driving down to the 20-yard line. Yale answered the punishing drive by pushing back forcefully, throwing Georgia for multiple losses and setting up a fourth-and-20 situation from the 30-yard line.

Wiehrs' number was called. But this time, he pulled up and lofted a pass to end Jack Curran down to Yale's 4-yard line. The bold, confident moved showed Georgia in attack mode, and the Bulldogs finished the job when fullback Jim Thomason

October 11, 1924

blasted into the end zone on a short dive. George Morton, who was fighting through injuries and questionable for the game, came on for the extra point and misfired his drop-kick. Georgia led 6-0 but knew leaving points on the field against Yale presented risks.

The defenses continued slugging each other in the second quarter. When Georgia stuffed a Yale drive, the Elis regained possession by forcing a fumble on their own 32-yard line. With Yale struggling to run against Georgia's stout defense, they resorted to more pass plays to even the score before halftime. This plan worked, to a degree, until Wiehrs intercepted Ben Cutler's pass at the Georgia 30, allowing Georgia to take its 6-0 lead into the locker room.

Yale, of course, never was going to abandon its run game with the talent it possessed on the line, even if the Southern Bulldogs spent the first half neutralizing its attack. To start the third quarter, Yale turned to reserve halfback Edmund Cottle. On eight of 10 plays, Cottle plowed downfield steadily, while mixing in a sharp 15-yard pass to Ducky Pond that set up Yale at Georgia's 20-yard line. Yale chipped away with a methodical drive into the teeth of Georgia's defense, and a Southern Bulldog penalty positioned Yale at the 3. From there, quarterback Eddie Bench powered into the end zone. Cottle was called to help finish what he started, and he booted the extra point for a 7-6 Eli lead.

Playing from behind, Georgia took to the air in the fourth quarter. A flurry of passes out of the backfield kept the Southern Bulldogs on the move, sparked by quarterback Andrew Moore's 50-yard connection to Curran down to Yale's 15-yard line. Cottle's fantastic tackle from behind

## Southern Bulldog, Northern Bulldog

prevented the touchdown, but Georgia was primed to take control of the game.

Yale's defense, however, delivered its statement. They stiffened after the aerial onslaught and suffocated Georgia's offense with rigid determination. Four downs later, Georgia had nothing to show for its efforts, opting to bypass a drop-kick field goal attempt.

Pinned deep in its own territory, Yale needed to muster a drive that resulted in points or bled the clock to nothing. Considering Georgia's defense had been immovable for large parts of the game, this was a significant challenge, even though Georgia center T. Roosevelt Day had been carried off the field with a severe leg injury and tackle Wesley Bass and guard Ike Joselove were injured.

Yale turned again to fullback Dan Allen, whose first-quarter run was one of the longest against the Southern Bulldogs, and reserve halfback Dan Lindley. The duo was up to the task. Snap after snap, Allen and Lindley gobbled up yards and kept the clock moving. Several successful running plays coalesced into a long, punishing drive that eventually wore down Georgia's tenacious defense. The Elis protected the ball and the Southern Bulldogs couldn't get the stop they needed. Time expired with Yale on Georgia's 3-yard line.

The battle was remarkably even. Yale totaled 218 yards rushing to Georgia's 216, and gained 13 first downs to Georgia's 12. Even the pass completions were nearly identical.

If Head Coach Woodruff believed in moral victories against Yale, especially after the shellacking of 1923, this was it.

October 11, 1924

*Raymond "Ducky" Pond earned his nickname from sportswriter Grantland Rice after a dashing performance in the rain against Harvard in 1923. Pond, an All-American halfback, played in the first two Yale-Georgia games and served as Yale head coach in the final game between the schools.*

Southern Bulldog, Northern Bulldog

# YALE

### STARTING LINEUP

Head Coach: T.A.D. Jones
Ends: John Bingham and Richard Luman
Tackles: Guy Richards and Benjamin Butterworth
Guards: Herbert Sturhahn and Richard Eckhart
Center: Winslow Lovejoy (Captain)
Quarterback: Edward Bench
Halfbacks: John Failing and Raymond Pond
Fullback: Daniel Allen

### SUBSTITUTES

Tackle: John Joss
Halfback: Edmund Cottle, Jr.
Guard: Richard Wortham, Jr.
Tackle: Reginald Root
Fullback: Henry Scott
Halfback: Benjamin Cutler
Guard: Stewart
Halfback: Daniel Lindley

October 11, 1924

# GEORGIA

## STARTING LINEUP

Head Coach: George "Kid" Woodruff
Ends: Jack Curran and Ralph Thompson
Tackles: N. James Taylor and J. Curtis Luckey
Guards: Ike Joselove and Ernest Rogers
Center: T. Roosevelt Day
Quarterback: Andrew Moore, Jr.
Halfbacks: Tom Nelson and Charles Wiehrs
Fullback: James Thomason

## SUBSTITUTES

Quarterback: George Morton
Halfback: Cecil Wyman Sherlock
Fullback: L.C. Randall
Tackle: Wesley Bass
Center: Martin Kilpatrick
Halfback: Armand Mapp
Halfback: Thomas Kain
Center: Carrol

Yale followed its win over Georgia with a tie against Dartmouth, a win over Brown and a draw with Army. The Elis then closed the season in fashion by dominating Maryland and picking up convincing wins over Princeton (10-0) and Harvard (19-6) for the second consecutive season. The 6-0-2 mark was a solid follow-up to Yale's national championship season of 1923. Richard Luman was named consensus All-American at the end position for 1924, and he served as captain of Yale's basketball team during the 1924-25 campaign. Ducky Pond, football captain Winslow Lovejoy, and John Joss earned All-American honors from various outlets, as well.

Georgia's stout defensive performance against Yale preceded a string of five consecutive shutouts over Furman, Vanderbilt, Tennessee, Virginia and Auburn. Woodruff's squad was in the hunt for a Southern Conference championship when the Bulldogs visited Alabama, which started the season with six shutout victories. Two of the South's strongest defenses took the field, but only one carried the day. The Crimson Tide blistered Georgia, 33-0, to earn its first Southern Conference title. The following week, Georgia lost a close game to Centre College, which handed Alabama its lone defeat, to cap a 7-3 campaign.

October 11, 1924

Yale's Richard Luman was an All-American end in 1924 and served as captain of Yale's basketball team in the 1924-25 season.

## OCTOBER 10, 1925

# YALE 35
# GEORGIA 7

### YALE BOWL
New Haven, Connecticut
Attendance 25,000

Heading into the 1925 season, Yale started to reconfigure its football program to be more in line with the university's overall academic mission, a pledge that Harvard and Princeton also made. Season-opening practice started later, and T.A.D. Jones' salary was to be reduced from $15,000 to $8,000 once his contract expired in 1926. This salary restructuring adhered to the new agreement that no coach be paid more than the school's leading professors.

## Southern Bulldog, Northern Bulldog

These decisions shaped Yale's transition from national football powerhouse to venerated Ivy League institution over the ensuing decades. But those changes didn't occur overnight, and there was plenty of football glory to gain while Yale remained a giant in the sport.

Against Georgia in 1925, Yale played like behemoths on a raw afternoon in New Haven.

The Elis tuned up with a 53-0 pasting of Middlebury, whose close games with Harvard in prior seasons attracted attention at Yale, while Georgia knocked off Mercer and lost a one-point decision to Virginia before traveling to Connecticut.

Georgia's starting lineup was overhauled from 1924, leaving inexperience on a defense that acquitted itself impressively. Yale captain John Joss battled a sinus infection severe enough to keep him out of the Middlebury game and away from the team for seven days. He saw his first action of the season as a substitute in the Georgia game.

Yale wasted no time capitalizing offensively. The Eli defense, meanwhile, stamped its imprint by intercepting four Georgia passes and smothering the Southern Bulldogs.

Yale blasted out of the gate in the first quarter. Halfback Ben Cutler sliced through Georgia's defense with swift end runs on the first two drives, setting up five-yard touchdown runs up the middle by halfback Billy Kline and fullback Dan Allen. In a blink, Yale led 14-0 and was just getting started.

On the opening drive of the second quarter, Allen orchestrated the attack with three lengthy runs that resulted

October 10, 1925

in Yale's third touchdown. The Northern Bulldogs took the ball back from Georgia and kept rolling. From midfield, Kline fired a 20-yard pass to end Walter Bradley, who sidestepped multiple defenders, shed tacklers, and bolted through Georgia for the remaining 30 yards and a touchdown.

Yale spent the rest of the quarter punting and pinning Georgia deep in its own territory to carry a 28-0 lead to the locker room. Georgia mustered three first downs in the half, mainly on a couple of 15-yard runs by halfbacks George Morton and William Hatcher before Yale defenders pulled them down from behind.

Yale's quick-strike offense and relentless defense recalled the Bulldogs' performance from two seasons prior, but Georgia committed to making a game of it. A steady attack opened the third quarter with Hatcher's 22-yard run and a long pass from Morton to Howell Hollis down to Yale's 38. Georgia had some momentum and needed points in a hurry.

Yale denied them. Four plays left Georgia short of the first down marker and Yale took over. Allen churned ahead for 21 yards, and then Bruce Caldwell boomed a punt inside Georgia's 5-yard line. The Southern Bulldogs tried another rally out of pride because the clock was winding down on the third quarter and the smash-mouth style didn't lend itself to quick scores.

Georgia's offense started to gather steam. Dashes around left end and off right tackle picked up 40 yards. A couple of pass plays sprinkled in, Moore to Morton and Hatcher to Hollis, swept the ball down to Yale's 5 where the Eli defense bared its teeth. Hollis gritted his and pounded through the

## Southern Bulldog, Northern Bulldog

middle of Yale's line to break the goal line and notch the lone touchdown. Then he added the drop-kick for good measure.

But Yale allowed nothing more. Fittingly, on a day when the Northern Bulldogs snatched so many Georgia passes, their final touchdown came when John Failing picked off a Morton pass and flashed 15 yards into the end zone for the game's final points.

Yale was back on strong ground in the rivalry, while Georgia's train ride to Athens left plenty of time for the Southern Bulldogs to ponder the school's worst start to a season since 1906.

October 10, 1925

Yale offensive lineman Herbert Sturhahn was a two-time All-American later enshrined in the College Football Hall of Fame.

Southern Bulldog, Northern Bulldog

# YALE

## STARTING LINEUP

| | |
|---|---|
| Head Coach: | T.A.D. Jones |
| Ends: | Frederick Potts and Walter Bradley |
| Tackles: | Guy Richards and Benjamin Butterworth |
| Guards: | John Flaherty and Reginald Root |
| Center: | Herbert Sturhahn |
| Quarterback: | Philip Bunnell |
| Halfbacks: | Benjamin Cutler and William Kline |
| Fullback: | Daniel Allen |

## SUBSTITUTES

| | |
|---|---|
| Halfback: | Bruce Caldwell |
| Guard: | Richard Wortham, Jr. |
| Halfback: | John Failing |
| End: | Stanley Gill |
| End: | Shattuck Osborne |
| Center: | David Burt, Jr. |
| Tackles: | John Joss (Captain) |
| Fullback: | James Wadsworth |
| Quarterback: | Dwight Fishwick |
| Halfback: | Edmund Cottle, Jr. |
| Halfback: | Louis Wienecke |
| Tackle: | Burt Benton |

October 10, 1925

# GEORGIA

### STARTING LINEUP

| | |
|---|---|
| Head Coach: | George "Kid" Woodruff |
| Ends: | Jack Curran and Ralph Thompson (Captain) |
| Tackles: | J. Curtis Luckey and E. Olin Huff |
| Guards: | Nathan Eubank and Hand |
| Center: | Jacob Butler |
| Quarterback: | Andrew Moore, Jr. |
| Halfbacks: | William Hatcher and Robert McTigue |
| Fullback: | Frank Boland, Jr. |

### SUBSTITUTES

| | |
|---|---|
| End: | Fowler |
| Fullback: | Tom Nelson |
| Halfback: | George Morton |
| Halfback: | Cecil Wyman Sherlock |
| Quarterback: | Howell Hollis |
| Fullback: | Dowess |
| End: | Luke Woodall |
| Quarterback: | John Broadnax |

After dominating Georgia, Yale dropped the next week's game against Penn. Though they later defeated Army, 28-7, the Elis' season fell well short of their mark for success. Yale closed the year with a loss to Princeton at Yale Bowl and a scoreless tie at Harvard for a 5-2-1 ledger. This also was the first year since Yale Bowl opened that the Elis played two road games. Typically, they alternated playing Princeton or Harvard on the road; in 1925, Yale accepted Brown's invitation to dedicate Brown Field on October 25 in Providence, Rhode Island. Individually for Yale, Sturhahn and Joss earned first-team All-American honors from various outlets.

Georgia rebounded from the Yale loss with consecutive wins over Furman and Vanderbilt before skidding in the second half of the season. The Bulldogs' lone win during the stretch came against Auburn, while they lost road games to Tennessee, Georgia Tech and Alabama. The Georgia Tech game, a 3-0 loss in Atlanta, was notable for being the first game between the schools since 1916 because of intense ill will – not surprising in a rivalry dubbed "Clean, Old-Fashioned Hate." The Bulldogs finished 1925 with a 4-5 record.

October 10, 1925

## OCTOBER 9, 1926
# YALE 19
# GEORGIA 0

### YALE BOWL
New Haven, Connecticut
Attendance 35,000

Defending the forward pass was Georgia's primary focus entering the fourth game in the series. Yale quarterback and captain Philip Bunnell had developed into a precise passer throughout 1925 and in the 1926 preseason. Georgia went to great lengths to devise a defensive strategy that could slow down Yale's newfound aerial attack, which produced five touchdown passes in a 51-0 win over Boston University to open the season. Such a display caused a stir in conservative Eastern football circles where the running game was deemed the superior strategy.

Georgia brought its own momentum to New Haven after dominating Mercer and Virginia in shutout victories to start the year. In pregame newspaper reports, experts predicted Georgia would turn to the passing game to keep pace with Yale. They were on the mark. Footballs certainly were flying at Yale Bowl in what became a record-setting day.

Georgia and Yale combined for the most total passes (30) and, in a nod to the defensive schemes created in anticipation, most incompletions (23) since Yale Bowl opened. Yale chalked up 115 yards passing, but Georgia captain George Morton also intercepted four passes and thoroughly impressed reporters covering the game. Georgia's aerial attack, however, never took off; all 10 attempts failed, either as harmless incompletions or Yale interceptions.

Immediately in the first quarter, Bunnell directed an aggressive Yale attack, spreading the ball to various receivers while the Bulldogs marched downfield. A short pass to fullback Lawrence Noble capped the drive with a touchdown.

Georgia's Morton struck back, leading a run-oriented drive during which he covered 60 yards personally. The Southern Bulldogs sought the equalizer and were in position to capitalize. But deep inside Yale's territory, defensive back William Kline intercepted Morton's lone pass attempt during Georgia's surge, ending it immediately.

Defense carried the second quarter. Georgia struggled to keep its offense on the field. Yale sputtered, too, before the Elis sustained a lengthy drive to the shadows of Georgia's goal

October 9, 1926

line. Here the Southern Bulldogs tightened up, and whether by a show of swagger or another reason, Yale eschewed a blast into the line by talented, powerful fullback Bruce Caldwell and instead chose to pass four times. All attempts failed in the face of Georgia's defense, and Yale settled for a 6-0 halftime advantage.

Yale was moving the ball through the air, but its failure to score from three yards out impelled the Northern Bulldogs to shift strategy in the third quarter. Their rushing attack flourished behind a line anchored by stalwart guard Herbert Sturhahn and Caldwell, a young workhorse who was destined for the National Football League after his days in New Haven.

Caldwell consistently pounded into and through Georgia's defense in the Elis' third-quarter drive, picking up yardage in chunks. Halfback Alfred Foote contributed with dives off center, all part of a long advance that Caldwell punctuated with a touchdown and a 12-0 lead.

Georgia, too, returned to its bread-and-butter run game in the second half, punching back and devouring yards. But when the Southern Bulldogs tried to mix up their attack with passes to keep Yale off guard, the plan backfired and Yale kept Georgia in check.

Yale's remaining drives revealed its versatility on offense. On one possession, the Northern Bulldogs covered 80 yards between Caldwell's rushes and Bunnell's passes to James Wadsworth. Georgia forced a fumble to stymie Yale, but the Southern Bulldogs couldn't generate any offense and their punt into a muscular wind died at Georgia's 20-yard line with the fourth quarter looming.

## Southern Bulldog, Northern Bulldog

At this point, Yale salted away the game by putting the ball in Caldwell's hands. Nothing fancy, just straight-ahead Yale football. Caldwell churned through the line play after play until he bulled his way into the end zone from six yards out. Wadsworth's point-after drop-kick made it 19-0.

Like the year prior, Georgia found itself playing for pride and attempting to avoid a shutout. The mighty Red and Black gathered a head of steam on the strength of backs William Hatcher, Herdis McCrary, Robert Hooks and William Noble, grinding through Yale's defense on two fourth-quarter drives. But fumbles ended both advances, and Yale sealed its victory.

While the passes flew at a dizzying rate, the running game proved most productive. Yale finished with 290 yards rushing, allowing it to control the clock and cap several drives with touchdowns. Georgia racked up an impressive 190 yards rushing, but the Yale defense stood firm near its goal line and thwarted the Southern Bulldogs' attack when it mattered most.

October 9, 1926

T.A.D. Jones is one of Yale's most decorated head coaches. He coached the Bulldogs during a successful nine-year career up to 1927. Jones then retired to teach at a prep school in New Hampshire and was inducted into the College Football Hall of Fame in 1958.

# YALE

## STARTING LINEUP

| | |
|---|---|
| Head Coach: | T.A.D. Jones |
| Ends: | Stewart Scott and Dwight Fishwick |
| Tackles: | Guy Richards and William Vadegrift |
| Guards: | Herbert Sturhahn and John Charlesworth |
| Center: | Charles Harvey |
| Quarterback: | Philip Bunnell (Captain) |
| Halfbacks: | Alfred Foote and William Kline |
| Fullback: | Lawrence Noble |

## SUBSTITUTES

| | |
|---|---|
| Fullback: | Earl Goodwine, Jr. |
| Fullback: | Bruce Caldwell |
| Quarterback: | Edmund Decker, Jr. |
| End: | Stuart Sanger |
| Halfback: | John Hoben |
| Tackle: | Sidney Quarrier |
| End: | James Wadsworth |
| Unknown position: | Ethan Hitchcock |
| Unknown position: | Burt Benton |
| Guard: | Graham |
| End: | Collins |

October 9, 1926

# GEORGIA

## STARTING LINEUP

| | |
|---|---|
| Head Coach: | George "Kid" Woodruff |
| Ends: | Tom Nash and Ivy Shiver, Jr. |
| Tackles: | Vernon Bryant and J. Curtis Luckey |
| Guards: | Ernest Rogers and Roy Jacobson |
| Center: | Walter Forbes, Jr. |
| Quarterback: | Roy Johnson |
| Halfbacks: | George Morton (Captain) and Cecil Wyman Sherlock |
| Fullback: | Frank Boland, Jr. |

## SUBSTITUTES

| | |
|---|---|
| Guard: | Lee Leffler |
| End: | Jack Curran |
| Tackle: | E. Olin Huff |
| Tackle: | Glenn Lautzenhiser |
| Halfback: | Robert Hooks |
| Halfback: | William Hatcher |
| Halfback: | Herdis McCrary |
| Halfback: | Fleming |

After defeating Georgia, the Elis notched a 14-7 win over Dartmouth to improve to 3-0. Then, they went into a tailspin with four consecutive losses, three of them by shutout. Of course, a win over Harvard makes any season successful, so Yale's 12-7 triumph in The Game was the redeeming moment, and the only one that mattered, in an otherwise pedestrian 4-4 campaign. Sturhahn earned All-American honors again, capping a career that led to his induction into the College Football Hall of Fame in 1981.

Georgia's loss to Yale caused a downward spiral the Bulldogs left unchecked until an emphatic victory over Florida on Halloween weekend. A shutout win over Auburn followed. Georgia secured a winning season with an all-important victory against Georgia Tech in Atlanta, 14-13, after trailing 13-0 at halftime, but closed their 5-4 season with a blowout loss at Alabama.

October 9, 1926

Bruce Caldwell, a decorated two-sport athlete at Yale, played in three Yale-Georgia games as a halfback and fullback. He later played professional football for the New York Giants and professional baseball for the Cleveland Indians and Brooklyn Dodgers.

## OCTOBER 8, 1927
# GEORGIA 14
# YALE 10

**YALE BOWL**
New Haven, Connecticut
Attendance 18,000

When Yale and Georgia clashed in 1927, both teams were destined for memorable seasons that remain important in their programs' histories. Observers caught a hint of their strengths during the October 1 opening weekend when Georgia blasted Virginia, 31-0, and Yale dominated Bowdoin, 41-0.

In an important development for Georgia in 1927, Head Coach Woodruff hired assistant Jim Crowley, former member of Notre Dame's famed Four Horsemen backfield, and he was

## Southern Bulldog, Northern Bulldog

instrumental in advancing the Bulldogs' proficiency within the Notre Dame running attack. Their first true test came against Yale.

On a cold and drizzly day in New Haven, Yale played sloppy football, losing a remarkable seven fumbles, while Georgia played a clean game and capitalized on the Elis' mistakes from the beginning.

In the first quarter, star halfback Bruce Caldwell coughed up the ball on Yale's 35-yard line. Georgia struck immediately with a quick drive capped by halfback Roy Estes' 12-yard touchdown catch and extra-point kick. Within five minutes of kickoff, the Southern Bulldogs led 7-0.

Five minutes later, Duncan Cox fumbled on Yale's 20 as Georgia threatened to build a big lead in the first quarter. Halfback Herdis "Bull" McCrary crashed ahead on four rushing attempts, powering the ball down to the 2-yard line. But here, Yale's defense dug in and stood up the Southern Bulldogs on four plays, the last an incomplete pass in the end zone, to halt the drive.

Late in the first quarter, Yale retaliated with a lengthy drive led by Caldwell, a decorated and unique athlete from gritty Cumberland, Rhode Island. His hard-charging runs, coupled with quarterback Johnny Hoben's dashes, kept the chains moving while Caldwell connected with end Stewart Scott for a 30-yard completion down to Georgia's 20. The combination worked so well Caldwell tried it again and zipped another pass to Scott for a 20-yard touchdown. Cox kicked successfully to knot the score at 7.

October 8, 1927

Yale mounted another drive early in the second quarter, powered by Cox's impressive 63-yard slashing run to Georgia's 17. Hoben and Caldwell again chipped away at the Red and Black's defense, edging down to the 2. Georgia forced fourth down and the ball went to Caldwell, bent on bulling his way through the line. But he lost the handle on the slick ball in the thick of Georgia's defenders, and the visitors recovered to escape damage.

Backed against his goal line, Georgia end and captain Chick Shiver punted out of trouble. Again, a steady rhythm of Caldwell and Hoben battering against Georgia's defense drove Yale into scoring territory. But the Southerners' defense held their ground, forcing Cox to attempt a 25-yard field goal that he booted through the uprights for a 10-7 Yale lead.

There was no slowing the back-and-forth affair in the first half. Georgia immediately commenced another long march propelled by a 50-yard pass from halfback Robert Hooks to Frank Dudley down to Yale's 7-yard line. From there, the bulldozer McCrary was called on to finish the drive, which he did by drilling his way over center and through the Yale wall. The point-after kick was eventful. H.F. Johnson Jr. booted the ball low and it ricocheted off a Yale lineman's head before clearing the crossbar by inches. Georgia 14, Yale 10.

With a four-point lead and halftime nearing, Georgia got the ball back and drove deep into Yale territory. On the final play of the half, Hooks looked for an advantage through the air, but Cox intercepted the pass and dashed the other way, desperate for a touchdown as the clock expired. Hooks never gave up on the play and gained on Cox, who kept motoring for the end zone. Hooks tracked Cox the length of

## Southern Bulldog, Northern Bulldog

the field and eventually dropped him 16 yards from pay dirt to preserve the Southern Bulldogs' 14-10 lead at the half. The play proved crucial as the game progressed.

The whirlwind first half impelled both coaches to substitute freely in the third quarter. Neither team moved the ball much and Georgia garnered only two first downs.

The game came down to the fourth quarter, and both squads bolstered their attacks with first-string talent. Yale leaned heavily on Caldwell, who had injured his ankle earlier in the game. The big back delivered and set the tone. He hammered repeatedly through Georgia's defense, running through left guard for large chunks of yards. Yale was moving the ball and threatening to overtake Georgia, but the Elis couldn't get out of their own way. Caldwell threw an interception near Georgia's goal line.

Three more times in the fourth quarter, Yale drove inside Georgia's 10-yard line. On the first attempt, Cox fumbled to kill momentum. The second drive ended at Georgia's 1 when the Southern Bulldogs bared their teeth and chased back Yale on downs.

A last-ditch Yale effort, with shadows creeping across the Bowl, drove the ball down to the 10. On a fourth-down play, quarterback George Loud dropped back and found Scott open in the end zone for the potential go-ahead score. Loud delivered the pass and Scott hauled it in, but Scott landed out of bounds to nullify the touchdown in an excruciating end for Yale.

On seven occasions, Yale drove inside Georgia's 10-yard

October 8, 1927

line without scoring and lost three fumbles in the fourth quarter alone as part of seven fumbles in the game. Georgia played a clean game and took care of the ball. Thus, Georgia secured its first victory over the mighty Northern Bulldogs and celebrations ensued.

As Whitner Cary wrote in his game report for the Atlanta Constitution, "A Georgia football team stepped into immortality" with the victory at Yale. Cary could not overstate the importance of the win, and he described joyfully the defensive stands Georgia's resolute unit delivered in the final five minutes of the game. "Those five minutes, gentle reader, are to me the outstanding picture as my tear-dimmed eyes watch the keys of this [typewriter]."

Yale was classy and gracious in defeat. T.A.D. Jones addressed the Georgia squad after the game, offering his congratulations, and mentioned Shiver, Nash and McCrary as among the finest at their positions to play at Yale Bowl. One unnamed Yale player said as he walked into the locker room, "We were beat by gentlemen whom it is a pleasure to play against."

Still, there was some sentiment among Yale men that the Northern Bulldogs defeated themselves with turnovers and an inability to execute near the goal line. Fair points, but Georgia fans, writers and many national college football observers would hear none of that.

Based on this victory and the whole of the 1927 season, Georgia fans created the rallying cry, "Georgia beat Yale; Yale beat Army; and the Army won the world war."

## Southern Bulldog, Northern Bulldog

Dick Hawkins, Atlanta columnist, noted the power shift that would change college football for generations to come. "The victory of Georgia in the aristocratic Yale Bowl is just one more step in a forceful campaign of convincing the world at large that Dixie can play at football along with the best. It's a hard pill for the northerners and easterners to swallow, but it is being rammed down their throats."

Georgia's victory made the Bulldogs a national name, a reality that Cary acknowledged at the end of his game report: "All glory to it!"
There was plenty of singing and rejoicing on the way home, which included a layover in New York for some sight-seeing before the Athens-bound train departed Penn Station.

Objectively, this game was the finest of the series for its equitable benefits. Both teams ultimately had reason to hold the 1927 campaign in high regard. Georgia earned its first win against Yale and finished with a claim to the national championship. Yale closed the season in strong fashion, its only loss to Georgia, and also laid claim to the national championship.

October 8, 1927

Yale All-American end Dwight Fishwick was part of the 1927 Northern Bulldog squad that captured the school's 27th and final national championship.

Southern Bulldog, Northern Bulldog

# YALE

## STARTING LINEUP

| | |
|---|---|
| Head Coach: | T.A.D. Jones |
| Ends: | Stewart Scott and Dwight Fishwick |
| Tackles: | Sidney Quarrier and Maxon Eddy |
| Guards: | Waldo Greene and William Webster (Captain) |
| Center: | Frederick Ryan, Jr. |
| Quarterback: | John Hoben |
| Halfbacks: | Bruce Caldwell and Edmund Decker, Jr. |
| Fullback: | Duncan Cox |

## SUBSTITUTES

| | |
|---|---|
| Center: | Arthur Palmer, Jr. |
| Quarterback: | Paul Switz |
| Halfback: | Earl Goodwine, Jr. |
| End: | Franklin Oldt II |
| End: | George Crile, Jr. |
| Center: | John Charlesworth |
| Halfback: | William Hammersley |
| Tackle: | Louis Ladd, Jr. |
| Fullback: | Knowlton Stone |
| Halfback: | Alfred Foote |
| Tackle: | Frank Marting |
| Guard: | Elmer Kell, Jr. |
| Quarterback: | Robert Hall |
| Quarterback: | George Loud, Jr. |

October 8, 1927

# GEORGIA

## STARTING LINEUP

Head Coach: George "Kid" Woodruff
Ends: Tom Nash and Ivy Shiver, Jr. (Captain)
Tackles: H. Cree Stelling and J. Robert Morris
Guards: Henry Smith and Roy Jacobson
Center: Joe Boland
Quarterback: John Broadnax
Halfbacks: Roy Estes and Robert McTigue
Fullback: Herdis McCrary

## SUBSTITUTES

Quarterback: H.F. Johnson, Jr.
Halfback: Frank Dudley
Halfback: Robert Hooks
Tackle: Theodore Frisbie
Fullback: Bennie Rothstein
Guard: Nixon
End: Collins

## Southern Bulldog, Northern Bulldog

The Dream and Wonder Bulldogs left New Haven poised to make history and earn national respect. Yale's 10 points scored were the most Georgia gave up all year. Its suffocating defense shut out the next five opponents (a streak that remains a school record) before Georgia scored convincing wins over Mercer and Alabama to earn the number-one ranking in the nation. The annual battle against Georgia Tech in Atlanta in early December attracted 38,000 fans to see the undefeated Bulldogs and one-loss Yellow Jackets, or Golden Tornado, as they were often known at the time, who had dropped a game at Notre Dame in October. Grant Field was a quagmire, and Georgia Tech slogged through the mud toward a 12-0 win that spoiled Georgia's perfect season.

Ivy "Chick" Shiver was an end and captain of the 1927 Dream and Wonder national champion Georgia Bulldogs, the first Georgia team to defeat Yale in the series.

While the defeat stung, it didn't derail Georgia's season in the history books. The Bulldogs were later named co-national champion with Yale, Illinois and Texas A&M. Head Coach Woodruff had announced earlier in the year his plans to retire from coaching and return to his lucrative insurance career in Columbus, and he went out on a high note.

Georgia's 1927 roster boasted remarkable star power. Tom Nash was named consensus All-American by Grantland

October 8, 1927

Rice, and he remained a two-sport star after his Georgia days. Nash became Georgia's first NFL player when he joined the Green Bay Packers in 1928 and contributed to three NFL championship teams through 1932, a season in which he earned First-Team All-Pro honors. He finished his career with the NFL Brooklyn Dodgers in 1933 and 1934. During this time, he also played minor league baseball.

*Tom Nash played the end position opposite Chick Shiver and created his own legacy in Georgia Bulldogs history. Grantland Rice named Nash a consensus All-American for his contributions to the 1927 national championship team.*

Other outlets bestowed All-American honors upon three more Dream and Wonder Bulldogs – Chick Shiver, a talented baseball player who later played for the Detroit Tigers and Cincinnati Reds, Gene Smith, and Herdis McCrary, who also went on to play with the Green Bay Packers.

For Yale, the 1927 national championship was the 27th and final claimed national championship for the proud program. Yale's defense never allowed as many points the rest of the season as the unit surrendered to the Southern Bulldogs. The Elis powered through four games against Brown, Army, Dartmouth and Maryland, winning by a combined 78-12,

## Southern Bulldog, Northern Bulldog

to set up the traditional year-end battles against Princeton and Harvard.

Yale was ready to make history. With its stifling defense and efficient offense, Yale knocked off Princeton (14-6) at Yale Bowl and Harvard (14-0) in Cambridge to close a remarkable year. As Woodruff moved on from Georgia after the season, so too did T.A.D. Jones leave after a history-making campaign and nine seasons leading the Northern Bulldogs. He then began his teaching career at Phillips Exeter Academy in New Hampshire, long a feeder school to Yale. Jones was inducted into the College Football Hall of Fame in 1958, a year after his death.

John Charlesworth and Bill Webster earned consensus All-American honors for Yale, while Dwight Fishwick, Stewart Scott and Sidney Quarrier were named All-Americans by other outlets. Bruce Caldwell earned All-American honors from various press associations, even though he was kicked off Yale's team late in the season. Yale officials, trying to control tramp football where players bounced around colleges, discovered Caldwell had played for Brown's freshman team a few years prior, and they removed him from the Bulldog roster. Caldwell stayed in New Haven and played on Yale's baseball team the following spring and displayed considerable talent. He went on to play with the 1928 Cleveland Indians for part of the season before joining the 1928 New York Football Giants for 10 games. He also played for the Brooklyn Dodgers in 1932 and logged 447 games in a minor league baseball career. During this time, Caldwell also was an entrepreneur, operating a smoke shop near Yale's campus, running a restaurant, acting as a boxing manager and co-owning various local sports teams. In 1955, he became a judge in West Haven Municipal Court 20 years after graduating from Yale Law School. He remains one of the most colorful figures in Yale sports history.

October 8, 1927

*Yale scores a touchdown in the 1927 game against Georgia. The Southern Bulldogs earned their first win over the Northern Bulldogs in this game, and both schools laid claim to the national championship at season's end.*

## OCTOBER 13, 1928
# YALE 21
# GEORGIA 6

**YALE BOWL**
New Haven, Connecticut
Attendance 25,000

Changes at the top gave the Georgia-Yale game a different flavor in 1928.

After several years as a Georgia assistant fine-tuning the Notre Dame shift in Athens, Harry Mehre took over as head coach in 1928 and began a 10-year run that lifted Georgia to national prominence. But in this game against Yale, there was little worth mentioning for the Red and Black.

Yale also introduced a familiar face as new head coach. Mal

Stevens, star halfback on the 1923 team, was 28 years old and college football's youngest head coach at a major school. When he wasn't running practices and strategizing on game day, Stevens taught orthopedic surgery at Yale Medical School.

Both schools won their October 6 season-openers in dominating fashion – Yale 27-0 over Maine and Georgia 52-0 over Mercer – before Georgia's contingent traveled the Seaboard Air Line Railroad up to New Haven where drizzly conditions left Yale Bowl's turf soggy for the game.

Determined to make a better showing than the previous year, Yale would need to do so without field general and quarterback Johnny Hoben, out with an injured tendon in his throwing arm. Head Coach Stevens tabbed Harlan "Hoot" Ellis as the fill-in starter.

No matter the quarterback, Yale's line was battle-ready, anchored by talented center John Charlesworth and captain tackle Maxon Eddy. From the opening possession, Yale flexed its muscles on the line, and the Northern Bulldogs maintained control through three quarters.

Georgia end Herb Maffett and tackle Theodore Frisbie took the brunt of Yale's forward marches, getting blasted off the line while fast and powerful halfback John Garvey chewed up yardage consistently. Those were the hallmarks of Yale's scoring drive in the first quarter, which resulted in a 22-yard Garvey touchdown run as he shed would-be tacklers at the goal line. Franklin Oldt II's point-after kick marked a 7-0 lead.

Georgia countered with a sustained drive, grinding out three first downs and advancing to Yale's 12-yard line. But the fumbles that plagued Yale a season prior cursed the Southern

October 13, 1928

Bulldogs in this moment, and the drive stalled. Yale recovered and punted away to force Georgia back in its own territory.

In the second quarter, Yale leveraged a 21-yard punt return by Ellis to Georgia's 24-yard line. The Red and Black countered with a strong defensive surge and forced a field goal attempt by Herbert Miller, Jr., which misfired. But Yale got a second life from an offsides penalty on the play, and the drive resumed in methodical fashion. The Northern Bulldogs pushed down toward Georgia's goal line before halfback Jacob Lampe burst through a hole off right tackle for the second touchdown, followed by the extra point.

Yale carried a commanding 14-0 lead into the locker room.

Nothing changed for Yale to start the second half. Its line continued to plow through Georgia's, and Garvey found wide paths as the feature back. His 19-yard run around left end, down to Georgia's 35, set up his next explosive run. Garvey tested the left side again and smashed through Georgia's wall, breaking tackles and stiff-arming defenders on his way to the end zone for the third time. Another successful kick gave Yale a 21-0 advantage.

Despite the uphill climb, Georgia fought on. The Southern Bulldogs sustained a long drive later in the fourth quarter and Frank Dudley bowled over for a short touchdown to put Georgia on the board. But the Bulldogs never threatened again, and Yale closed out a strong victory.

Many Yale followers claimed the 1927 Georgia win was a fluke and used this 21-6 result as proof that Yale remained superior. Their argument would crumble under Georgia's dominance over the next five years.

Southern Bulldog, Northern Bulldog

# YALE

## STARTING LINEUP

| | |
|---|---|
| Head Coach: | Marvin Stevens |
| Ends: | Franklin Oldt II and John McEwen III |
| Tackles: | Frank Marting and Maxon Eddy (Captain) |
| Guards: | Elmer Kell, Jr. and Robert Spiel |
| Center: | John Charlesworth |
| Quarterback: | Harlan Ellis |
| Halfbacks: | John Garvey and Edmund Decker, Jr. |
| Fullback: | Chauncey Hubbard |

## SUBSTITUTES

| | |
|---|---|
| Halfback: | George Loud, Jr. |
| Guard: | Arthur Palmer, Jr. |
| End: | George Crile, Jr. |
| Fullback: | Kempton Dunn |
| End: | Daniel Hickok |
| Guard: | Ralph Miner |
| Center: | Frederick Loeser, Jr. |
| Halfback: | Herbert Miller, Jr. |
| Halfback: | Jacob Lampe |
| Tackle: | Louis Ladd, Jr. |
| Quarterback: | Robert Wilson |
| End: | Hulbert Aldrich |
| Tackle: | McCalmont |

October 13, 1928

# GEORGIA

### STARTING LINEUP

| | |
|---|---|
| Head Coach: | Harry Mehre |
| Ends: | Herbert Maffett and Vernon Smith |
| Tackles: | Theodore Frisbie and Glenn Lautzenhiser (Captain) |
| Guards: | Roy Jacobson and Eugene Haley |
| Center: | Joe Boland |
| Quarterback: | H.F. Johnson, Jr. |
| Halfbacks: | Frank Dudley and B. Harvey Hill |
| Fullback: | Herdis McCrary |

### SUBSTITUTES

| | |
|---|---|
| Halfback: | Robert Hooks |
| Guard: | E. Olin Huff |
| Fullback: | Bennie Rothstein |
| End: | Henry Palmer |

Yale won the following week against Brown for a 3-0 start before descending into an irreversible tailspin in Stevens' first season. The Elis dropped four of their final five games to finish 4-4, including losses at Princeton and against Harvard. Guard Waldo Greene, who didn't play against Georgia, earned All-American honors.

Georgia recovered from the Yale loss with three consecutive wins (Furman, Tulane, Auburn) and fashioned a strong 4-1 mark by early November. But the Southern Bulldogs derailed at the end with four losses to finish Mehre's first season 4-5.

October 13, 1928

John Charlesworth earned All-American honors as a standout center on the 1927 Yale team and also starred for the 1928 squad.

# THE INVITATION

Dr. Steadman Vincent Sanford envisioned a magnificent new football stadium for the University of Georgia, one that would be the envy of the South and, especially, Georgia Tech. When he announced his intentions, he encouraged fans and alumni to sign notes guaranteeing a bank loan in exchange for lifetime seats to Georgia games. The people responded enthusiastically, supporting a $150,000 loan to start construction.

Again, Georgia looked to Yale for inspiration. Sanford hired North Carolina-based engineer and architect Thomas C. Atwood, an MIT graduate who served as lead engineer on Yale Bowl's construction, to oversee the project and create a smaller version of Yale Bowl in Athens. Before leading the Georgia stadium project, Atwood was involved in several major engineering projects in Boston and Philadelphia and oversaw the University of North Carolina's major expansion in the 1920s, including Kenan Memorial Stadium, which opened in 1927.

## Southern Bulldog, Northern Bulldog

Ground broke for Georgia's stadium in 1928 near the site of the old Sanford Field, in a natural valley between Old Campus and the university's Agricultural School. The site was ideal for constructing seats that rose up the hills and looked down upon a field soon to be encircled by its signature privet hedges.

With his vision becoming a clearer reality by the day, Sanford extended his formal invitation to the one institution that would bring dignity, honor and familial respect to the stadium's first game.

## The Invitation

Athens, Ga., September 28, 1928

Doctor George H. Nettleton. Chairman
Yale University Athletic Association,
Yale University.
New Haven, Conn.

My dear Doctor Nettleton:

When Chief Justice Taft, then president-elect, honored the University of Georgia by a short visit, he was struck by the familiar outlines of a building called "Old College." He was informed that when the building was constructed in 1805, the blueprints were obtained from Yale college.

Franklin College, which is the college of arts and sciences, was founded by Abram Baldwin; its first president, Josiah Meigs, and all of its early professors were Yale graduates; and it is evident that, in some way, they inculcated the spirit which has become traditional in both institutions. In the early days of Georgia, everything in the institution was deliberately modeled on Yale usages. In a very peculiar way, therefore, this institution has always felt its kinship with Yale; though it would perhaps be extravagant to paraphrase a well-known title and speak of "Yale-in-Georgia."

When it was determined to build an athletic stadium, it was quite natural that we should turn to the man who built the Yale Bowl. Mr. Atwood is now constructing a smaller stadium, but one which will be worthy of comparison, except in size. We are exceedingly proud of our ambitious effort, and are eager to have the stadium dedicated with proper formality, and to make the occasion memorable because of the fame of the team which dedicates it.

Among all the institutions which we meet, there is none which so fully measures up to our desires as Yale. In addition to the ordinary considerations, there would be a strong feeling of that sentiment which plays so large a part in a proper college spirit. The unfailing courtesy which our boys have received at Yale has aroused the deepest feeling among our people, and we covet the opportunity of repaying it in kind, if not in degree. It would give the people of Georgia, who would gather in great numbers, an opportunity to see one of the great teams of the country, and could not fail to impress them most happily.

    We therefore most earnestly and cordially invite Yale to honor us by dedicating the new stadium, October 12, 1929, the date of the Yale-Georgia game in 1929, or on some date which will be agreeable to the institution.

                    Very respectfully,

                    S. V. Sanford
                    Dean of the University of Georgia.

## The Invitation

New Haven, Conn., October 26, 1928.

Dean S. V. Sanford
University of Georgia,
Athens, Georgia.

My dear Dean Sanford:

    It is my pleasant duty and privilege to inform you that the board of control of the Yale University Athletic Association at its first meeting of the current academic year has gratefully accepted your friendly proposal that the Georgia-Yale football game on October 12, 1929, be played at the new Georgia stadium as the occasion of its dedication. Our board recognizes with satisfaction the close academic and athletic connections between the two universities and the exceptional circumstances which your invitation generously emphasizes. The continuance of the Georgia-Yale game on its usual date and its transfer for the coming season to the Georgia stadium will, we trust, confirm and strengthen the cordial relations which already exist.

    With assurance of our high regard, I am
        Faithfully yours,
            (signed) GEORGE H. NETTLETON

    Chairman of the Board of Control Yale University Athletic Association.

Mal Stevens, left, was a standout back for Yale and later became head coach for several seasons. Waldo Greene served as Yale's team captain in 1929 under Stevens, the first Yale team to play a game in the Deep South.

## OCTOBER 12, 1929
# GEORGIA 15
# YALE 0

### SANFORD STADIUM
Athens, Georgia (Stadium Dedication Game)
Attendance 35,000

Yale visits Athens, Georgia. In the modern day of jet-setting college football teams, the magnitude of this event can go unappreciated. Once Yale Bowl was completed in 1914, Yale did not travel for more than one game each year, and that was only against Princeton or Harvard. Further, Yale had never played a game in the Deep South before the Athens trip. Prior to 1929, the farthest south Yale played a game was Annapolis, Maryland, against Navy. Certainly, prestige and pride factored in. This was Yale, and Yale dictated where and when it played football. Additionally, many administrators and influential alumni believed far-flung football games on Saturday distracted from the university's academic priorities and compromised a football player's educational experience. This loud chorus of opinion led Yale to shape its football program into an element of campus life more complementary to the academic mission as the sport of college football continued to grow into a massively popular money-making machine throughout the country.

Georgia asking Yale to visit Athens for a football game was akin to asking the royal family over for tea when they rarely left the palace. Yale was the royal family, but its administration also held a deep fondness for the University of Georgia. Yale made an exception that it never would have for another southern institution, because of the universities' historical connection and mutual affection.

Therefore, when the mighty Northern Bulldogs of Yale arrived in Athens aboard the Yale Special, Athens became host to a multi-day carnival for college football fans, influential politicians and business leaders, society folk and the generally curious. Athens' civic leaders viewed the game as a referendum on the city's ability to host such a massive event and willingness to invest in infrastructure for similar weekends in the future. Majestic Sanford Stadium now beckoned in this city of 15,000 residents.

As former Bulldog Head Coach Kid Woodruff said, "That old highway, even when it is paved through, will be inadequate to handle the crowds between Atlanta and Athens. When Georgia folks watch one game from that great new stadium, nothing will keep them away."

October 12, 1929

Nearly 50 special trains arrived from New York, Chicago, Washington and cities and towns throughout the Southeast, including Atlanta, whose trains offered riders sandwiches from the famous Pig'n Whistle restaurant. More than 50 airplanes landed at the local airfield during the weekend and more than 5,000 people arrived by car. The increased traffic helped spur investment in Athens, and the Chamber of Commerce hosted a manufacturers' display during the week of the game that attracted large crowds of people interested in learning about Athens industry and local products.

All of Athens was dressed up for the affair and everyone sought a party, just two weeks before the Wall Street Crash of 1929 upended their lives. Mayor A.G. Dudley and the city council led the movement to decorate city streets, public buildings and local business fronts in red-and-black and blue-and-white bunting, pennants and banners. The Athens Garden Club urged homeowners to beautify their properties leading up the game, and the club added markers around town that introduced visitors to places of historic interest.

A large group of students and faculty from the University of Georgia met the Yale train and escorted them uptown in a joyful procession. The schools' bands paraded through the streets paying homage to the other – Yale's band playing "Dixie" and Georgia's playing "Boola Boola" – mixed with other traditional marches to delight the crowds that packed the sidewalks. Tea parties, dances and country club dinners popped up all over town, and newspapers published society notes about hosts and hostesses and the esteemed guests they entertained.

Visitors filled hotels in Athens and nearby towns. Residents opened their homes, and many Athenians hosted open houses throughout the weekend, serving sandwiches and coffee.

In his welcoming address to the visitors from New Haven, Georgia Governor Lamartine Griffin "L.G." Hardman said, "My friends, yours are the keys to Georgia's homes. We will give you everything we've got except one thing – the football game."

The event wasn't just Georgia's. It attracted people from all over the United States and as far south as Cuba, all paying $3 apiece for a ticket. Some arrived as part of travel groups sponsored by alumni chapters and others as individual witnesses to one of college football's most remarkable moments in the South. Georgia Tech alumni requested 1,000 tickets, Clemson alumni spoke for 250, and Atlanta-based alumni clubs of Princeton and Dartmouth requested blocks of 50 tickets. For people who didn't descend on Athens, NBC Radio broadcast the game nationally.

So important was Yale's arrival in the Deep South that several other college football teams shifted their games to Friday afternoon or night to free their schedules for Saturday's battle in Athens. The Atlanta area, especially, was awash in a wave of football excitement. Georgia Tech moved its game against North Carolina to Friday afternoon at Grant Field and many of the dignitaries due in Athens spent Friday in Atlanta. In Montgomery, Florida and Auburn played under flood lights on Friday night, as did Clemson and North Carolina State in Florence, South Carolina. Ten other southern games also were switched to Friday in deference to Georgia-Yale. The historic tilt transcended football and became an Athens social event without equal.

October 12, 1929

Before boarding the train in New Haven, Yale President James Rowland Angell captured the spirit of the event from his university's perspective.

"Superficially considered, the Georgia expedition might appear to be an invasion in force of the territory of a hostile folk. In point of fact, it is an embassy of good-will…We should never think for a moment of sending a Yale team on a 500-mile expedition merely to play a football game. [I]t has seemed to us appropriate to show our Georgia friends the high regard in which we hold them by sending our team and other official representatives to assist in the dedication of their new stadium."

With that, Angell was on his way to greet his contemporary, Dr. Sanford. As an interesting aside, Yale's four-man golf team also traveled to Athens for a Saturday morning match against Georgia before all attended the football game.

On Sanford's proposal, Georgia's General Assembly and Governor Hardman marked game day as Abraham Baldwin Day, an official holiday named in honor of the University of Georgia's first president. Hardman welcomed multiple politicians to Athens: House Majority Leader John Q. Tilson of Connecticut; Connecticut Governor John H. Trumbull, who attended the game shortly after his daughter, Florence, and former President Calvin Coolidge's son, John, got married in late September in a Plainville, Connecticut, ceremony that attracted national attention; first-term New York Governor Franklin D. Roosevelt, who spent his winters in Warm Springs, Georgia, and was in town to root for the Southern Bulldogs; North Carolina Governor O. Max Gardner; Alabama Governor Bibb Graves, a Yale graduate; Florida Governor Doyle E.

Carlton; and South Carolina Governor John G. Richards.

Sanford entertained Angell, University of North Carolina President H.W. Chase, Vanderbilt President J.J. Tigert and many business leaders of the day, including John J. Pelley, president of the New York, New Haven & Hartford Railroad who became a Georgia fan when he presided over the Central of Georgia Railroad.

The game's wide appeal created several months of build-up in the national media and highlighted Athens and the University of Georgia in a manner never experienced. By the time Yale weekend arrived, journalists were noting that Athens was "no longer a bashful little city," as Dan Magill of the Atlanta Constitution put it, and everyone now knew about the home of the Southern Bulldogs.

Yale's traveling group stayed in the center of the party at the Georgian Hotel on East Washington Street, a few blocks north of Sanford Stadium, and occupied the entire fifth floor. A detective from Athens' finest manned a post by the elevator to ensure only Yalies and their escorted guests had access during the wild weekend.

Athens was electrified like never before, but all the while, residents stayed true to themselves and their everyday routine. Taxi drivers charged their regular 50 cents from the train station to any hotel and carried the luggage inside; hoteliers charged normal rates for rooms, still served full breakfasts for 75 cents and apologized that meals were fixed and not offered a la carte; uptown restaurants poured 5-cent coffee and stacked 10-cent sandwiches; football banners sold for 15 and 25 cents. No one took advantage of the event to

October 12, 1929

gouge visitors.

Quarts of alcohol (beer, liquor or maybe even moonshine) were going for four and five dollars each. The uncertainty of the drinks in the street might have caused the Yale Athletic Association to print a warning at the bottom of its players' itinerary cards: "Players must only drink special bottled water."

Athens rolled out the welcome mat for Yale. In signature Southern style, three women of distinguished backgrounds were selected as official sponsors to greet and support Yale during the weekend: Josephine Hollis of Atlanta, Cynthia L'Engle of Jacksonville, Florida, and Penelope Cannon of Cannon, North Carolina. The Atlanta Constitution published lengthy stories about their patrician backgrounds and society connections.

While Yale lodged in the center of festivities and revelry, Georgia's Harry Mehre removed his team from downtown Athens to spend a quieter night before the game in the university's farmhouse at the agriculture school south of town.

By 8 o'clock on game day morning, Athens' streets and hotel lobbies were jammed with people eager to keep the parties going another day. Yale's band played a concert on a lawn next to the Georgian Hotel and attracted a huge crowd. A newspaperman from Atlanta also remarked how yo-yos, a new craze in the 1920s, captivated Yale men and young girls alike who bought them from Athens' dime stores, adding to the street-carnival atmosphere. One local florist arranged bunches of violets for Yale and red roses for Georgia and sold them to young men eager to impress women.

## Southern Bulldog, Northern Bulldog

Around noon, Georgia's 80-piece band lined up in front of the Georgian Hotel and jubilantly launched into "Dixie" while leading fans in a march toward the stadium and mixing in some Yale songs along the way. Yale's 50-piece band soon joined the pregame party, and the Yale team left the hotel at 12:15 to walk to Sanford Stadium.

Many people in Athens that day had never seen anything like Sanford Stadium, nestled in a natural amphitheater with a forest of Georgia pine at one end and an open green field at the other, packed to capacity, with another 500 spectators sitting on the hill above the rim on the south side. Flags for Yale, Georgia and other Southern schools flew above the main entrance while the American flag was flanked by Georgia's and Connecticut's state flags beyond the end zone.

A program of pregame festivities awaited the fans with performances by both schools' bands. Just before kickoff, in a crowning moment, a group of Georgia alumni presented Dr. Sanford with a $1,500 gold cup to express their gratitude for his vision and execution of the plan that created what many were calling the finest football stadium in the South.

After all the pageantry, football was to be played on a warm autumn afternoon that felt more like summer, with women wearing Chantilly dresses and men wearing shirtsleeves.

Leading up to the game, the Southern Bulldogs stumbled out of the gate with a 13-6 loss to Oglethorpe on September 28, followed by a 28-0 win over Furman. Yale opened its season by annihilating Vermont, 89-0, using a series of deft fake-handoff plays with Albie Booth scurrying everywhere.

October 12, 1929

Yale Head Coach Mal Stevens was implementing a new offensive system with two wingbacks in 1929, mixing the Notre Dame shift, Pop Warner's offense and hybrid variations. He hired Adam Walsh, an All-American center for Knute Rockne, to coach the line in '29 and help ingrain the system. Walsh ended up staying in New Haven until 1933 when he moved to Harvard, then Bowdoin, and eventually landed in professional football where he coached the Cleveland Rams to the 1945 NFL Championship.

Looking at the matchup on paper, experts pegged Yale as a three-touchdown favorite after its staggering win over Vermont. Georgia immediately proved a different animal with a stout defense, especially at the heart of its line with captain Joe Boland and heralded guards Ralph "Red" Maddox and Milton "Red" Leathers, both known by their hair color.

The teams spent the first quarter getting a feel for the game and each other's tendencies, trading punts while the ball primarily stayed in Georgia's territory as Yale consistently pressured punter Vernon "Catfish" Smith. Late in the quarter, Yale fumbled one of Smith's kicks and Georgia recovered on Yale's 46. The Elis stiffened and forced a punt, but field position had shifted.

*Catfish Smith, who played end, is a University of Georgia football legend – key figure in the 1929 win over Yale, consensus All-American in 1931 and member of the College Football Hall of Fame.*

In the second quarter, Georgia angled to get the first serious opportunity after Armin Waugh returned a punt 12 yards to Yale's 35. From there, the Southern Bulldogs went to work. Weddington Kelley, Georgia's end, made a remarkable catch on a sharp pass with two Yale defenders in front of him to get down to the 20-yard line. Waugh then raced off left end for an eight-yard run. The Elis' line stood firm. Frederick Loeser and Daniel Hickok burst through and tackled Georgia runners for losses, and the Southern Bulldogs eventually turned the ball over on downs.

After its defensive stand, Yale planned to punt away on first down to flip the field. But playing two quarters in the Georgia heat and absorbing the Southern Bulldogs' advances left Yale's linemen breathing heavily. On the punt attempt, a swarm of Georgia linemen cracked Yale's front and Robert Rose blocked Donald McClennan's kick. The ball ricocheted into the end zone and Catfish Smith fell on it for the first score, whipping the Sanford Stadium crowd into a frenzy. Smith added the extra point for a 7-0 lead.

Yale countered by calling on Booth, a sophomore from Milford, Connecticut, who soon became a Yale legend known as "Little Boy Blue." The slithery, 145-pound halfback tied defenses in knots and left the opposition grasping at air. The Georgia game was his first significant varsity action with the Elis, and he was eager to make his mark. Yale's ensuing drive covered significant yardage on the ground, and Booth's 18-yard scamper was a highlight. Georgia pushed back and eventually held Yale at the Southern Bulldogs' 30-yard line. Booth faded back to the 38 to try a drop-kick field goal, but it

fell well short of the mark for a touchback. The half ended with Georgia leading 7-0.

October 12, 1929

A photo of one of the most iconic plays in Georgia football history: Catfish Smith recovers a blocked punt for a touchdown in Georgia's 15-0 win over Yale in 1929 during the dedication game for Sanford Stadium.

The defensive stalemate and field-position battle continued in the third quarter. Smith pinned a fine punt out of bounds at Yale's 12-yard line to put the pressure on the Northern Bulldogs. On the next play, the offense's signals got mixed up and the snap from center sailed past Booth before he was ready. While the ball bounced perilously toward his team's goal line, Booth gave chase and scooped it up in the end zone. By that time, Georgia's speedy, aggressive linemen, led by Smith, were on top of Booth and smothered him for a safety, and a 9-0 advantage.

Sanford Stadium was rocking jubilantly, a concentration of all the energy from the week leading up to this moment. Fueled by the crowd, Georgia continued to apply pressure after Yale's kickoff, which fullback Jack Roberts ran back into

Eli territory. For the rest of the period, the Southern Bulldogs were on the move, and it took a fine defensive play by Booth, who swatted away a fourth-down pass, to keep Georgia at bay during the early stages of the fourth quarter.

Yale was desperate for offensive momentum in the final quarter, and, naturally, Booth generated it, starting with a booming punt back to Georgia's 30-yard line. Austin Downes fielded the kick and promptly fumbled. Yale captain Waldo Greene picked up the loose ball without breaking stride and raced in for an apparent touchdown to give Yale a needed jolt. However, a rule change for the 1929 season prohibited the kicking team from recovering and advancing a fumbled punt, and the ball came back to the 30 where Greene had taken possession.

Booth promptly went to work. He shot through the right side of the line for a splendid 16-yard run. Several crashes into and through Georgia's wall took the ball down to the 6 to force a fourth-down situation. For Yale, a touchdown would be a boon, turning the one-sided contest into a one-possession game. But Georgia's flinty defense repelled the advance and squelched Yale's fourth-down attempt to maintain momentum.

Still, Yale wasn't finished. It forced a Georgia punt and turned to its passing game for answers. A few attempts clicked and carried the Northern Bulldogs inside Georgia's 20. But Smith, the do-everything Georgia end on this day, stamped his mark in another big way when he intercepted a lateral pass. Smith punted back to Yale to flip the field, and Georgia's defense came through again. This time, Bennie Rothstein intercepted a pass near midfield and returned it to Yale territory.

October 12, 1929

After another Georgia punt, Yale set up for more aerial attacks as time slipped away. The Northern Bulldogs were trying everything to advance, but another errant throw found its way into Georgia hands – the third interception of the fourth quarter.

Georgia started at Yale's 30 and wasted little time cementing victory in this historic game. Two short runs set up one final, definitive play. Halfback Spurgeon "Spud" Chandler, future right-handed pitcher for the World Series Champion New York Yankees, lofted a beautiful pass toward Smith, who hauled in the spiral at the 13-yard line and cruised untouched into the end zone to finish the 28-yard scoring play.

It was an artful ending to a milestone day for Georgia football. An ecstatic crowd rushed the field after the victory and all of Athens celebrated wildly in the streets deep into the night.

Booth had introduced himself to the college football world, and he would soon awe spectators with his elusiveness, exhibiting fluid jukes and sidesteps that eventually landed him in the College Football Hall of Fame. But he was unable to break out against a Georgia defense that tackled sharply.

In the final tally, Yale gained more first downs than Georgia, but the Southern Bulldogs executed the biggest plays of the game at the most opportune times, sealing a victory that rang out nationally. In some people's minds, Georgia's win transcended the sport. The Atlanta Constitution's editorial board called October 12, 1929, "one of the most memorable and pleasurable days in the history of the state."

In their postgame reports, several writers noted the warm

and sunny Georgia afternoon, more like early September in New England, took a toll on Yale men wearing heavy, dark blue jerseys. Robert F. Kelley of the New York Times claimed, "There is no doubt that Yale suffered badly from the heat." The Northern Bulldogs substituted generously, sending in five and six players at a time to the point the scorer couldn't keep track. Postgame reports from Atlanta discussed how much weight Georgia players lost during the battle, proving weather affected all players.

After the game, Yale Head Coach Mal Stevens offered no excuses, only gratitude.

"We played our very best, but the Georgians had the better team today," Stevens told Kankakee Anderson of the Atlanta Constitution. "We have been given a fine reception down here and even though we didn't win, we have thoroughly enjoyed our stay."

October 12, 1929

# GEORGIA

### STARTING LINEUP

| | |
|---|---|
| Head Coach: | Harry Mehre |
| Ends: | Vernon Smith and Weddington Kelley |
| Tackles: | Robert Rose and Theodore Frisbie |
| Guards: | Ralph Maddox and Milton Leathers |
| Center: | Joe Boland (Captain) |
| Quarterback: | Austin Downes, Jr. |
| Halfbacks: | Marion Dickens and John Davidson |
| Fullback: | Bennie Rothstein |

### SUBSTITUTES

| | |
|---|---|
| Halfback: | Armin Waugh |
| Fullback: | Jack Roberts |
| Center: | Spero Tassapoulas |
| Halfback: | Spurgeon Chandler |
| End: | Herbert Maffett |
| Tackle: | Vernon Bryant |

October 12, 1929

# YALE

## STARTING LINEUP

| | |
|---|---|
| Head Coach: | Marvin Stevens |
| Ends: | Daniel Hickok and John Walker |
| Tackles: | Frank Marting and Francis Vincent |
| Guards: | Frederick Loeser and Waldo Greene (Captain) |
| Center: | Arthur Palmer, Jr. |
| Quarterback: | Robert Wilson |
| Halfbacks: | Charles Snead and Herbert Miller, Jr. |
| Fullback: | Kempton Dunn |

## SUBSTITUTES

| | |
|---|---|
| Halfback: | Donald McLennan, Jr. |
| Guard: | T. Truxton Hare, Jr. |
| Quarterback: | Albert Booth |
| Halfback: | Albert Taylor |
| Fullback: | David Austen |
| Halfback: | Harold Cruikshank |
| End: | Herster Barres |
| Tackle: | Robert Hall |
| Guard: | Frederick Linehan |
| Center: | Samuel Gwin, Jr. |
| Halfback: | Lindenberg |

## Southern Bulldog, Northern Bulldog

Georgia's 1927 team thrust the program into the national spotlight, and the 1929 squad solidified its position as a burgeoning force beyond the Southeast. Hosting Yale in the Sanford Stadium dedication game was a monumental event in Athens, and Georgia was on its way to becoming a long-standing power. A few years after this historic win, Georgia joined the Southeastern Conference (SEC) as a charter member, contending for conference and national championships ever since.

Besides playing Yale, Georgia ventured to New York City in 1929 to battle the powerful New York University Violets at Yankee Stadium, further increasing the Southern Bulldogs' exposure in different parts of the country. Georgia held their own with NYU before falling, 27-19. Any disappointment from that loss dissipated quickly over the next three weeks with victories over Auburn, Alabama and Georgia Tech to close a 6-4 season. Individually, Catfish Smith impressed national voters and earned All-American honors.

Although its loss in Athens reverberated nationally, Yale notched notable victories over Army and Princeton in ensuing weeks, sandwiching a tie with Maryland. The only loss after Georgia was bitter and season-ending, though – at Harvard to close a 5-2-1 season. Three Elis earned All-American honors: captain Waldo Greene, Albie Booth and Herster Barres.

October 12, 1929

Halfback Spud Chandler threw a 28-yard touchdown pass to Catfish Smith to seal Georgia's famous 15-0 win over Yale in 1929. He later threw nearly 1,500 innings as a New York Yankees pitcher, winning 109 games and three World Series rings.

Southern Bulldog, Northern Bulldog

## FAY VINCENT'S ITINERARY CARD
### for Yale's historic trip to Athens, Georgia

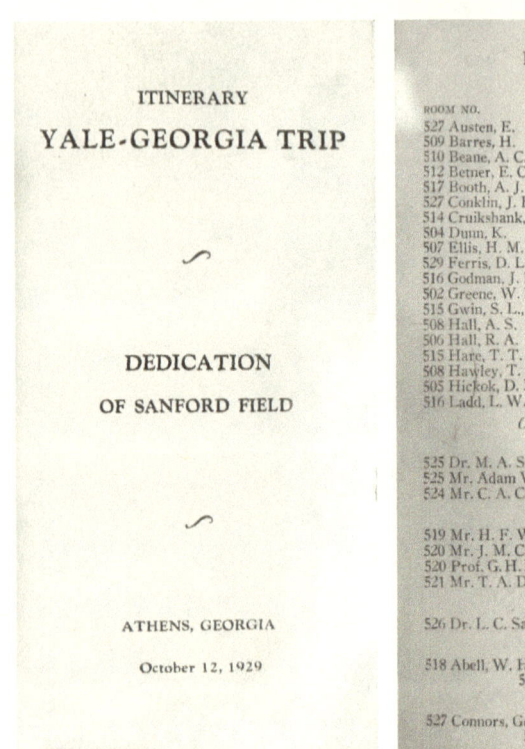

Front      Back

October 12, 1929

## ITINERARY

NAME **VINCENT, F.T.**
CAR **501**
SECTION **Lower 11**
HOTEL ROOM **529**

### Thursday, October 10

(All men bring suitcases to Y Club at Lunch)

- 2:00 P.M. Buses leave Athletic Office for R. R. Station.
- 2:30 P.M. Yale - Georgia Football Special leaves New Haven.
- 4:30 P.M. Train arrives New York.
- 4:35 P.M. Train leaves New York.
- 6:00 P.M. DINNER—Players eat in Private Diner.
- 6:30 P.M. Officials, Coaches and Trainers eat in Private Diner.
- 9:55 P.M. Arrive Washington.
- 10:10 P.M. Leave Washington.
- 10:15 P.M. All Players in bed.

### Friday, October 11

- 8:00 A.M. BREAKFAST—Players.
- 8:30 A.M. Rest of the Party.
- 12:30 P.M. LUNCH—Players.
- 1:00 P.M. Rest of the Party.

- 3:00 P.M. Arrive Athens, Georgia. (Party will be taken to Georgian Hotel in cars. LEAVE BAGS TO COMPETITORS.
- 3:30 P.M. Walk to Sanford Field.
- 4:00 P.M. Practice. (Walk to Hotel Georgian after practice.)
- 6:30 P.M. DINNER for Players and rest of Football Party by University of Georgia at Country Club.
- 10:00 P.M. All Players must be in bed.

### Saturday, October 12

- 8:30 A.M. BREAKFAST—Every one eat in Private Dining Room on Second Floor.
- 11:30 A.M. LUNCH—Players eat in P. D. R.
- 12:15 P.M. Leave Hotel for Field House. Walk in group.
- 1:45 P.M. DEDICATION OF SANFORD FIELD.
- 2:00 P.M. Game called.
- 6:00 P.M. SUPPER in P. D. R. Hotel Georgian. (BRING SUITCASES TO P. D. R. AND VACATE ROOMS BEFORE SUPPER.)
- 9:00 P.M. Special Train leaves Athens.

### Sunday, October 13

Every one eat à la carte in Private Diner. (Competitor will o.k. checks.)
- 9:30 P.M. Train arrives New Haven.

*PLAYERS MUST DRINK ONLY SPECIAL BOTTLED WATER*

Inside

### Sunday, October 13

Every one eat à la carte in Private Diner. (Competitor will o.k. checks.)
9:30 P.M. Train arrives New Haven.

**PLAYERS MUST DRINK ONLY SPECIAL BOTTLED WATER**

*Tackle Fay Vincent served as captain of the 1930 Yale football team and 1931 Yale baseball team, one of only three Yale athletes (with Malcolm Aldrich and Larry Kelley) to hold the captaincy in both sports. Vincent was a key member of the 1929 team that made the historic trip to Athens, Georgia, to dedicate Sanford Stadium.*

OCTOBER 11, 1930

# GEORGIA 18
# YALE 14

**YALE BOWL**
New Haven, Connecticut
Attendance 45,000

On the heels of the historic 1929 game, Georgia and Yale engaged in another memorable battle in New Haven in 1930. Both teams were strong, and Georgia boasted plenty of speed. There was no question of either team's talent after Yale notched a 38-0 win over Maine and 40-13 conquest of Maryland while Georgia dominated Oglethorpe (31-6) and Mercer (51-0) to start the season.

In typical Georgia fashion, the Southern Bulldogs dug in and thrived on their physical running game behind a crew of

## Southern Bulldog, Northern Bulldog

bruising linemen. Yale, with dazzling playmaker Albie Booth and a stout line anchored by captain Fay Vincent, offered plenty of resistance.

The Southern Bulldogs made an emphatic opening statement. Austin Downes, wearing a red number 1 on his white jersey, took the kickoff and disappeared into the scrum before he shook loose and flashed out into the open field. The footrace was on, and Downes sprinted toward pay dirt. No Yale player could touch him, and 81 yards later, Georgia led 6-0.

The thrill of that first play faded quickly for Georgia, though, as Yale's defense refused to budge and never allowed Georgia a first down in the entire half. But the Elis found Georgia's defense just as stubborn. Yale twice drove deep into Georgia territory during the opening quarter, but the offense stalled on a fourth-down incomplete pass and again after a fourth-down sack.

The teams traded punches in this heavyweight fight before Booth kickstarted the attack, as was his nature, in the second quarter. The highlight was a 35-yard pass Booth threw to halfback Alpheus Beane, Jr. down to Georgia's 16-yard line. From there, Yale chipped away with short-yardage runs, aided by a Georgia penalty. Booth got the call once more, and the shifty back climbed over and scampered around defenders in a tight space to jam the ball over the goal line from four yards out. He added the extra-point kick for a 7-6 lead. The Booth-to-Beane combination nearly worked again during another second-quarter drive, but a pass slipped through Beane's fingers in the end zone.

Georgia was desperate for any offense, and reserve halfback

October 11, 1930

Spud Chandler gambled with a pass deep in his own territory late in the second quarter. Yale's defense trumped him with an interception and return down to the 21-yard line to set up a last-second field goal attempt. Booth lined up a kick to give his team a boost, but he misfired wide and Yale held its one-point lead going into halftime.

Yale kicked off to Georgia to start the second half, and Georgia end Weddington Kelley received the ball deep in his territory before Yale's Vincent hit him hard to force a fumble at the 18-yard line. Herster Barres alertly scooped up the fumble in stride and raced into the end zone for a dramatic touchdown; then, he kicked the extra point for a 14-6 advantage.

*Herb Maffett was captain of the 1930 Georgia Bulldogs and earned All-American honors from various outlets.*

Of course, the rules prohibited the kicking team from advancing a fumbled ball – and a similar play was correctly adjudicated the year prior – but Georgia captain Herb Maffett never challenged the call and the play stood.

After slamming repeatedly into a stone wall for an entire half, the Southern Bulldogs had plenty of work to do. They started with a variety of deceptive plays to augment their straight-ahead attack. Georgia's backfield of Marion Dickens, Spud Chandler and James Stoinoff cracked

Yale's front with change-of-direction runs, delayed passes and quick handoffs through the heart of the defense, leading to the Southern Bulldogs' first substantial gains of the afternoon.

The Southern Bulldogs hadn't relied much on the passing game, but Chandler let it fly in Yale territory. On one play, Crowley tipped a pass in the defensive backfield, but Catfish Smith was in the right place, even though he was on the ground. The ball fell into Smith's lap at Yale's 26-yard line. Dickens burst through the guard hole for 15 yards on the next play, setting up a prime opportunity for Georgia. Ultimately, they fumbled it away.

Georgia continued to pressure Yale, its defense shutting down the Northern Bulldogs and forcing a punt that set up Georgia at the Yale 39. From the previous drive, Georgia knew it was on to something and employed the same mix of plays. Georgia picked up a chunk of yards for a first down at Yale's 25, and then Chandler capped off the drive properly. He found Smith on a crossing route, and the talented end hauled in the pass and took it the distance for a touchdown that cut Yale's lead to 14-12.

Yale countered. A lengthy drive positioned the Elis on Georgia's door step, forcing the Southern Bulldogs to respond at a critical point late in the third quarter. They measured up, hunkered down, and stuffed Yale on four downs.

Momentum was going Georgia's way, particularly early in the fourth quarter when Chandler recovered a Yale fumble around midfield. Georgia returned to its power running game. Halfback Buster Mott burst ahead for 26 yards. Fullback Jack

October 11, 1930

Roberts blasted through the line for nine more. A costly Yale penalty placed the ball at the 4-yard line and backed its defense into a corner.

They scrapped like seasoned fighters, turning back successive running plays and gearing up for another goal-line stand. Roberts of Georgia, however, seized the moment. On third down, the fullback barreled into the fatigued Yale line and broke through to the end zone for the go-ahead score.

Yale had time to rally, and Booth provided the spark. He took the ensuing kickoff and jetted upfield for 36 yards. For most of the afternoon, Georgia's defense bottled up Booth and didn't surrender any of his trademark long runs. They also delivered physical messages to the 145-pound back and kick returner, twice getting flagged for unnecessary roughness when tackling him. One of those penalties occurred on this kickoff return, and the ball moved up to midfield for Yale with about three minutes to play.

The Elis were in solid position for a dramatic ending, but Georgia had its own plans. On the snap of the first play, Chandler dropped into coverage in the defensive backfield and read a pass. The ball came his way and he quickly snatched it for Georgia's third interception of the day, sealing the come-from-behind victory.

In the end, Yale gained more first downs than Georgia, 15 to 9, but the Southern Bulldogs' defense stopped Yale on downs four times to thwart scoring opportunities and forced four turnovers. The performance provided Georgia's offense enough opportunity to figure out a strategy that worked against Yale's tough defense in the second half.

Southern Bulldog, Northern Bulldog

# YALE

## STARTING LINEUP

| | |
|---|---|
| Head Coach: | Marvin Stevens |
| Ends: | Lindenberg or Lindberg (spelled both ways) and Herster Barres |
| Tackles: | Robert Hall and Francis Vincent (Captain) |
| Guards: | T. Truxton Hare, Jr. and Frederick Linehan |
| Center: | Frederick Loeser |
| Quarterback: | Donald McLennan, Jr. |
| Halfbacks: | Patrick Sullivan and Kempton Dunn |
| Fullback: | Joseph Crowley |

## SUBSTITUTES

| | | | | |
|---|---|---|---|---|
| End: | John Madden | | Tackle: | Thomas Hawley |
| Quarterback: | Charles Heim | | Center: | John Walker |
| Quarterback: | Albert Booth | | End: | John Sargent |
| Halfback: | Alpheus Beane, Jr. | | End: | Hans Flygare |
| | | | Fullback: | Walter Levering |
| Halfback: | Albert Taylor | | Halfback: | James Conklin |
| Fullback: | John Muhlfeld | | Halfback: | David Austen |
| Guard: | James Stewart | | Tackle: | Arthur Hall |
| End: | Edward Doonan | | Guard: | Connor |

October 11, 1930

# GEORGIA

## STARTING LINEUP

| | |
|---|---|
| Head Coach: | Harry Mehre |
| Ends: | Vernon Smith and Herbert Maffett (Captain) |
| Tackles: | Robert Rose and Jim Hamrick |
| Guards: | James Patterson and Jasper Bennett, Jr. |
| Center: | Spero Tassapoulas |
| Quarterback: | Austin Downes, Jr. |
| Halfbacks: | Spurgeon Chandler and Marion Dickens |
| Fullback: | James Stoinoff |

## SUBSTITUTES

| | |
|---|---|
| Guard: | Ralph Maddox |
| End: | McCarthy Crenshaw |
| Fullback: | Jack Roberts |
| Halfbacks: | Norman Mott |
| End: | Weddington Kelley |
| Center: | J. Vason McWhorter, Jr. |
| Tackle: | Edward Davis |
| Fullback: | Lynn |

## Southern Bulldog, Northern Bulldog

After the Yale game, the Southern Bulldogs continued a strong march through their schedule with convincing wins over North Carolina (26-0) and Auburn (39-7), a scoreless tie with Florida and an impressive 7-6 win at New York University. In the Southern Conference, Alabama and Tulane stood atop the standings and both schools shut out Georgia in November. The Bulldogs rescued their season with a 13-0 win over Georgia Tech in Atlanta to finish 7-2-1. Two Georgia players earned All-American honors from various outlets – end Herb Maffett and guard Ralph Maddox – while guard Red Leathers (who didn't play in the 1930 Yale game), fullback Jack Roberts and end Catfish Smith made the All-Southern team for a Bulldog squad that many at the university considered the most talented to date.

Yale moved on from the Georgia loss to fashion a solid record through November with ties against Army and Dartmouth and a 10-7 win at Princeton. But the Bulldogs couldn't get past Harvard at Yale Bowl, dropping a 13-0 decision for their third consecutive loss to the Crimson since winning the 1927 national championship. Yale finished 5-2-2. Albie Booth and Frederick Linehan were named All-Americans.

October 11, 1930

Austin Downes provided the jolt in the 1930 Georgia-Yale game by returning the opening kickoff 81 yards for a touchdown in New Haven. In 1931, Downes earned recognition on All-American lists.

### OCTOBER 10, 1931
# GEORGIA 26
# YALE 7

**YALE BOWL**
New Haven, Connecticut
Attendance 70,000

A capacity crowd at Yale Bowl in early October served as a gorgeous backdrop for the ninth meeting between the two Bulldogs. Rarely had the famous Bowl hosted such a mass of football fans so early in the season. For Georgia, this was the first of three games played in front of crowds of at least 63,000 in 1931.

Both teams took care of business convincingly in their openers – Georgia crushed Virginia Tech, 40-0, and Yale cruised past Maine, 19-0. The Southern Bulldogs arrived in New Haven without Head Coach Harry Mehre, who was in Indiana with his ailing father, and first-year assistant Rex Enright served as head coach. The temporary change in leadership had no adverse effect on the visitors.

Yale's coaching staff had undergone an interesting change, too, when Head Coach Mal Stevens hired former University of Michigan and New York Giants star Bennie Friedman as an assistant.

Georgia played with a distinct chip on its shoulder and laid it on Yale after its second-string unit turned in an eventless first quarter. With the first-stringers on the field in the second quarter, Georgia kicked into gear, starting on defense.

Yale halfback Albert Taylor dropped back, forced to elude attacking Georgia defenders who were hanging on him, and flicked his pass toward a receiver. Lineman Red Leathers fought off his blockers, extended his hands and intercepted the pass, running 40 yards downfield for an electrifying touchdown. Georgia led 6-0 after the kick failed.

On the kickoff, Yale's dynamic playmaker Albie Booth took the ball at his 6-yard line and rocketed into the scrum. Suddenly, he emerged unscathed with only two defenders, including Austin Downes, between him and the equalizer. Downes played an angle that slowed Booth enough for Georgia's kick coverage to catch up and tackle Booth at the 19-yard line after a 75-yard return.

Tempers flared after the whistle, and Georgia fullback Jack Roberts and Yale tackle John Wilbur nearly started a fistfight

## October 10, 1931

before the referee intervened and ejected both players. The Northern Bulldogs were in solid position, but they wasted Booth's explosive return and eventually gave up the ball on downs.

Georgia made one more surge toward the end of the first half, and it was demoralizing for Yale's defense. With the ball on its own 27-yard line after a punt, Georgia had time for a final desperation play with house money. The call went to quick and elusive halfback Homer Key, running a sweep around left end. The wall of Georgia blockers bowled over Yale defenders so decisively that Key raced 73 yards, untouched, for a touchdown that sent a surge through Georgia supporters. Wendell Sullivan kicked the extra point and Georgia went into the locker room with a convincing 13-0 advantage.

Yale had plenty of time to recover, and the Northern Bulldogs took emphatic steps early in the third quarter after Georgia fullback Buster Mott fumbled on his own 33-yard line. Entered the irrepressible Booth, whose deftness with run and pass plays carried the Elis downfield and set up his short touchdown toss to end Herster Barres. Booth's kick cut Georgia's lead to 13-7, which held until the fourth quarter.

When Yale got the ball back, Georgia's defense imposed its will again. As Booth dropped back to punt, the line broke and a swarm of defenders pressured the All-American into a shanked kick that went out of bounds at Yale's 28-yard line. Georgia gained 16 yards on the ground to set up a 12-yard touchdown pass from Downes to Key. Catfish Smith converted the kick for a 20-7 Georgia advantage.

Later in the quarter, Marion Dickens intercepted another Yale pass near the Elis' 40. Behind its strong line and determined rushing attack, Georgia pounded its way downfield. Fullback Lloyd Gilmore's short-yardage blast into the end zone capped the scoring.

Georgia overpowered Yale for large parts of this game. The Southern Bulldogs rushed for 258 yards, passed for 80, and logged 13 first downs while holding Yale to 114 total yards and only four first downs. Two interceptions, one returned for a touchdown, kept Georgia in control for much of the day.

To close the afternoon, Yale's band played "Dixie" as a goodwill gesture to Georgia, the only team other than Harvard to defeat Yale in three consecutive years at that point.

Halfback Marion Dickens returns a kick in the 1931 game at Yale Bowl played before 70,000 fans. Dickens, who intercepted a pass late in the game, played a key role in Georgia's 26-7 win.

October 10, 1931

Ralph "Red" Maddox (left) teamed with Milton "Red" Leathers (right) to form a powerful guard duo for the Georgia Bulldog teams of 1929-31. They shared a nickname based on their hair color.

Southern Bulldog, Northern Bulldog

# YALE

## STARTING LINEUP

Head Coach: Marvin Stevens
Ends: Hans Flygare and Herster Barres
Tackles: John Wilbur and Arthur Hall
Guards: Albert Strange and Edward Rotan II
Center: Edward Doonan
Quarterback: Robert Parker
Halfbacks: Joseph Crowley and Albert Taylor
Fullback: John Muhlfeld

## SUBSTITUTES

Halfback: Albert Booth (Captain)
Fullback: Walter Levering
Tackle: John Kilcullen, Jr.
Tackle: Joseph Uihlein
Guard: William Saner
Center: Benjamin Betner
End: John Sargent
Guard: Alan Converse, Jr.
Quarterback: Patrick Sullivan
Halfback: Robert Lassiter, Jr.
Halfback: Kay Todd, Jr.
Quarterback: Harold Sandberg
Center: Hillman Holcombe

Guard: Edward Nichols
Tackle: Gilbert Wright
Tackle: Franz Ingelfinger
Guard: Douglas MacArthur II
Fullback: Hughes
End: Moore

October 10, 1931

# GEORGIA

### STARTING LINEUP

| | |
|---|---|
| Head Coach: | Rex Enright |
| Ends: | McCarthy Crenshaw and Louis Wolfson |
| Tackles: | E.C. Townsend and William "Bull" Cooper |
| Guards: | James Patterson and Jasper Bennett, Jr. |
| Center: | Graham Batchelor |
| Quarterback: | Wendell Sullivan |
| Halfbacks: | Spurgeon Chandler and Norman Mott |
| Fullback: | Joseph Whire |

### SUBSTITUTES

| | | | |
|---|---|---|---|
| End: | Weddington Kelley | End: | Fred Miller |
| Guard: | Ralph Maddox | Halfback: | Sam Brown |
| Fullback: | Jack Roberts | | |
| Guard: | Milton Leathers | | |
| Halfback: | Marion Dickens | | |
| End: | Vernon Smith | | |
| Tackle: | Robert Rose | | |
| Tackle: | Jim Hamrick | | |
| Halfback: | Homer Key | | |
| Fullback: | Lloyd Gilmore | | |
| Center: | J. Vason McWhorter, Jr. | | |
| Quarterback: | Austin Downes, Jr. (Captain) | | |

## Southern Bulldog, Northern Bulldog

Mal Stevens ensured Yale recovered quickly and decisively after losing to Georgia. The Elis shut out the University of Chicago and St. John's of Maryland, then tied Army (6-6) and Dartmouth (33-33) to set up the annual showdowns among the Big Three. Yale got the best of both opponents in a hard-fought 3-0 win at Harvard and a 51-14 conquest of Princeton, which still stands as the largest win in this rivalry for either school. Eli All-Americans included Herster Barres and Albie Booth, his third such recognition during his Yale tenure.

Georgia continued to roll through its schedule after pulling out of New Haven on the southbound train. The Bulldogs picked off three Southern Conference opponents before riding back up to New York City to knock off NYU, 7-6, in front of 63,000 fans at Yankee Stadium, after which fans tore down the goalposts and brought pieces back to Athens on the team train. Georgia, undefeated after six games and considered the best team in the country, then dropped an important home tilt to Tulane, eventual Southern Conference champion and Rose Bowl participant.

Georgia recovered to beat Auburn and paste Georgia Tech, 35-6. The Bulldogs then ventured to Los Angeles to face powerhouse USC, coached by the legendary Howard Jones, former Yale player and coach. Georgia had tested Northeast markets and fared well, but Los Angeles was a different story in 1931. The Trojans whipped Georgia, 60-0, before 75,000 fans at Los Angeles Coliseum on December 12 to close Georgia's season at a respectable 8-2 against a brutal schedule of strong teams. The two teams responsible for the Bulldogs' losses met in the Rose Bowl a few weeks later, with USC knocking off Tulane to claim the national championship.

Catfish Smith was a consensus All-American and fellow Bulldogs Red Leathers and Austin Downes earned recognition on additional All-American lists.

October 10. 1931

Albie Booth, known as Little Boy Blue, hailed from nearby Milford, Connecticut, and thrilled Bulldog fans for several years with his electrifying runs and elusiveness. Only 5-foot-6 and 144 pounds, Booth was named to All-American teams every year he played for Yale's varsity and later was inducted into the College Football Hall of Fame. He served as captain of Yale's 1931 team.

# 1932

## No Game Played

In the middle of the Great Depression, Georgia and Yale scaled back their schedules and paused the rivalry for Yale to host the University of Chicago in its only intersectional game. Georgia kept a train trip to the Northeast on its schedule, traveling to New York City to battle the NYU Violets in a 13-7 loss. Both Bulldogs' seasons were forgettable. Yale finished 2-2-3 and Georgia 2-5-2. Head Coach Mal Stevens stepped away from Yale's varsity team after 1932. He later became NYU's head coach, while teaching orthopedic surgery classes at the school, before becoming a noted surgeon in the New York metropolitan region.

Reggie Root, left, is one of many Yale players who later became head coach of the Bulldogs. He coached Yale's freshman team in 1932 before taking over the varsity program in 1933. Root, a former offensive lineman, is seen with 1933 captain and halfback Bob Lassiter.

### NOVEMBER 11, 1933

# GEORGIA 7
# YALE 0

---

### YALE BOWL
New Haven, Connecticut
Attendance 35,000

For the first time in the series, the Georgia-Yale game took place in November instead of the second or third week in October.

Another change occurred in Yale's leadership. Former Yale lineman Reggie Root, who coached the freshman team the year prior, took over the varsity program from Mal Stevens, who became freshman coach in 1934 to devote more time to his medical school teaching. Offensively, Yale switched to the Notre Dame style offense for 1934 because Root had Notre Dame men as assistant coaches focused on the line and backfield. New York Times sportswriter Allison Danzig called the strategy switch proof that Root was "one of the smartest and most resourceful young men in the coaching profession…"

Root's debut season started with wins over Maine, Washington & Lee and Brown, before a 21-0 loss to Army preceded a 14-13 win over Dartmouth. At 4-1 going into the Georgia game, Yale looked as strong as the New York press believed it would be in the preseason. However, the new offense was a concern; Yale hadn't scored more than 14 points in a game and was winning on the strength of its defense.

Head Coach Harry Mehre, meanwhile, ran his talented Southern Bulldogs through the first six games undefeated, and with relative ease. The closest decision was 13-12 over Mercer, and Georgia shut out New York University and Florida in the two weekends prior to riding the train to New Haven. Georgia also became part of the newly formed SEC in 1933, a pairing that has stood the test of time amidst super-conference upheaval in college football, and probably always will.

By this point in the rivalry, Georgia was separating itself from Yale. A UPI writer claimed Georgia was favored by six touchdowns in this game, and a New York Times correspondent expressed surprise that Yale played its Southern visitors so closely in a clean game that featured no turnovers.

The 1933 version of Georgia-Yale was a throwback to the previous decade – a smash-mouth spectacle with few forward passes. Yale rushed for 197 yards and passed for 38 yards on

November 11, 1933

six completions; Georgia, meanwhile, gained 272 of its 273 total yards on the ground, led by elusive 145-pound halfback Homer Key and his 125 yards. Combined with thundering fullback George Chapman and a stout line, the Southern Bulldogs' running game was in peak condition.

Georgia marched steadily on its opening drive and threatened Yale's end zone. Key powered the drive with a 41-yard run, and the Southern Bulldogs pounded down to the goal line. But Yale's defense saved the Elis, stiffening and keeping Georgia out of the end zone on four downs.

Georgia got the ball back in the first quarter after a lengthy Yale punt and set up another attack. Key tore through the Northern Bulldogs with another long run, covering 38 yards and breaking inside Yale's 30. Georgia continued to dent Yale's defense and moved within three yards of the goal line. That's when Chapman got the call and bowled his way through for a touchdown, followed by Joseph Grant's extra point, to cap a 67-yard drive.

Neither team could solve the opposing defense in the second quarter, and they traded punts until halftime.

Yale came out strong in the third quarter in search of the equalizer and suddenly found cracks in Georgia's armor. Halfback Bill Keesling picked up 27 yards on two carries to bring the ball to midfield before Richard Cummins (lost for the season with a knee injury later in the game) connected with Jerome Roscoe on a 20-yard pass play. Keesling carried down to the 14 and Yale had all the momentum.

In this moment, Georgia's defense exhibited the mettle that

produced three shutouts so far in the season. When Yale hammered into the line, Georgia repelled them. When the Elis went to the air, the Southern Bulldogs shot them down. Four plays left Yale outside the end zone, and Georgia took over.

Another third-quarter drive stalled for Yale inside the Georgia 20-yard line after a series of successful runs by fullback Earl Nikkel. Whatever Yale tried, Georgia ultimately answered defensively. The fourth quarter played out like the second, a series of punts trying to create better field position for the offense, but neither side gained an advantage.

The final gun sounded on a 7-0 Georgia win. Yale's defense did all it could, never allowing Georgia inside its 25-yard line after the touchdown. Georgia's defense did a little bit more.

Though they were outnumbered among the 35,000 in attendance, Georgia fans spilled onto the field and splintered Yale's goal posts for souvenirs. Fistfights broke out and police intervened to clear the field as emotions ran high.

November 11, 1933

Graham Batchelor served as captain of Georgia's powerful 1933 team that started the season 7-0 following a win at Yale Bowl in November.

Southern Bulldog, Northern Bulldog

# YALE

## STARTING LINEUP

| | |
|---|---|
| Head Coach: | Reginald Root |
| Ends: | Richard Herold and Bernard Rankin |
| Tackles: | John Kilcullen, Jr. and Francis Curtin |
| Guards: | Paul Grosscup and Horace Davis II |
| Center: | Victor Malin |
| Quarterback: | Thomas Curtin, Jr. |
| Halfbacks: | Robert Lassiter, Jr. (Captain) and William Keesling |
| Fullback: | Andrew Callan |

## SUBSTITUTES

| | |
|---|---|
| Guard: | Richard Crampton |
| Halfback: | Richard Cummins |
| Quarterback: | Jerome Roscoe |
| End: | John Overall, Jr. |
| Fullback: | Earl Nikkel |
| Center: | Laurence Goodyear |
| Guard: | James DeAngelis |
| Guard: | Edward Nichols |
| Halfback: | Stanley Fuller |
| Fullback: | Robert Childs |
| End: | Coombs |

November 11, 1933

# GEORGIA

## STARTING LINEUP

| | |
|---|---|
| Head Coach: | Harry Mehre |
| Ends: | Charlie Turbyville and Graham Batchelor (Captain) |
| Tackles: | Charles Opper and John West |
| Guards: | David McCullough and John Brown |
| Center: | Tom Perkinson |
| Quarterback: | Byron Griffith, Jr. |
| Halfbacks: | Homer Key and Joseph Grant |
| Fullback: | George Chapman |

## SUBSTITUTES

| | |
|---|---|
| Fullback: | Marion Gaston, Jr. |
| Fullback: | Joe Crouch |
| Guard: | Leroy Moorehead |
| Tackle: | Allen Shi |
| Halfback: | Sam Brown |

## Southern Bulldog, Northern Bulldog

With a 7-0 record, Georgia suffered a disappointing letdown the week after its New Haven trip, losing to Auburn for its only setback in SEC play. The Bulldogs recovered with their fourth win in five games over Georgia Tech (including a tie in '32) to set up a rematch with USC in Los Angeles on December 2. The Trojans were as inhospitable in 1933 as they were two years prior, blasting the Bulldogs, 31-0, to end Georgia's 8-2 season. USC and Georgia didn't play each other again until 1960 (a 10-7 USC win in Los Angeles) and haven't since.

Yale's defeat set the stage for blowout losses to Harvard and Princeton, compelling influential alumni to threaten a financial boycott of the football program. Pressure intensified, and Head Coach Root was forced out after a 4-4 mark in his only varsity coaching season at Yale.

November 11, 1933

Homer Key was a 145-pound halfback who regularly slipped through and raced around Yale defenders during Georgia's win at Yale Bowl in November 1933.

Larry Kelley was a sophomore on Yale's 1934 team, the last squad to play Georgia. Kelley soon became an All-American and the Bulldogs' first Heisman Trophy winner.

NOVEMBER 10, 1934
# GEORGIA 14
# YALE 7

**YALE BOWL**
New Haven, Connecticut
Attendance 25,000

Alumni unrest forced a change that ushered Raymond "Ducky" Pond, among the legion of notable Yale stars, into the head coach's position. In his first season, Pond and his Northern Bulldogs were tested immediately by a schedule that college football writers called the most difficult in school history against eight major programs. The season-opener was a home game against Lou Little's Columbia Lions, a team that defeated Stanford in the previous year's Rose Bowl, laid claim to a share of the 1933 national championship and returned plenty of high-caliber talent. Easing into the season with opening games against Bates and Maine was a thing of the past.

Pond's first order of business was to scrap the Notre Dame offense of '33 and return to the single-wing attack reminiscent of the T.A.D. Jones era. Pond also hired Earl "Greasy" Neale as one of his assistants, a decorated former professional football and baseball player who became a Hall of Fame head coach of the Philadelphia Eagles after his stint at Yale. Notable assistants Denny Myers, former Chicago Bear guard, and Ivy Williamson, captain of Michigan's 1932 national championship team and future Wisconsin coach, rounded out the new staff.

Head Coach Mehre provided continuity at Georgia as he entered his seventh season, and the '34 edition of the Southern Bulldogs promised to be stronger than the previous year's. Their record eventually proved the point, but they stumbled to a .500 mark heading into Yale Bowl with a rare non-conference loss to North Carolina and SEC setbacks at Tulane and Alabama – ultimately, the conference's co-champions.

Yale managed a 3-2 mark before the Georgia game, propped up by wins over Penn, Brown and a high-powered Dartmouth eleven. Columbia and Army handed the Bulldogs two losses. The 7-2 win over Dartmouth gave Yale fans confidence going into the Georgia game.

November 10 was bitter in New Haven, cold and gray with hints of a New England winter in the air. It was a day suited for stingy defenses and strong running games, which both schools fielded.

November 10, 1934

Yale landed the first blow in the opening quarter. With the ball on his own 32-yard line, Eli quarterback Tommy Curtin took the snap for a running play with Georgia in immediate pursuit. A smooth sidestep left defenders clutching air, and Curtin raced up the sideline for 21 yards. Fullback Stanley Fuller got the call on the next play. He hammered into Georgia's line, off left guard, with locomotive power and burst into the second level of the defense. From there, it was a foot race, and Fuller outran Georgia's secondary en route to a 47-yard touchdown. With captain and guard Francis "Clare" Curtin's point-after-touchdown kick, Yale stunned Georgia with a 7-0 lead.

The Southern Bulldogs took possession and ignited their vaunted ground attack behind all-SEC linemen John Brown, guard, and John McKnight, center. Georgia churned up to midfield before Yale's defense forced halfback John Bond, soon to become the best quick-kicker in Georgia's history, to punt deep into Yale territory. The Elis kicked it back immediately and Georgia started on Yale's 42.

The Red and Black employed a series of reverses and fake reverses aimed at opening holes in Yale's left side while Brown, McKnight and guard Frank Johnson mauled inside. This strategy drove the ball down to Yale's 22 but, again, the Northern Bulldogs held strong and took over.

Yale had turned back two solid Georgia drives, and Tommy Curtin was ready to go to work again. He called his own number on the first play and turned to push upfield. But as he fought for yardage, Georgia's defense jarred the ball loose and recovered on Yale's 26-yard line, creating a prime opportunity for the offense to strike.

They didn't waste it. Two plays later, speedy halfback Al Minot raced through an open hole, hurdled two defenders and swiftly covered 24 yards into the end zone. Bond booted the extra point to tie the game.

Yale mustered another strong drive in the second quarter. Tommy Curtin took to the air in search of sophomore end Larry Kelley, future Heisman Trophy winner. The duo connected on a fine pass and Kelley broke free into Georgia's open field before Byron Griffith hauled him down from behind at the 30-yard line. The next play was a lateral to halfback Stratford Morton and he swept forward for a 12-yard gain. Some grinding ahead and a Georgia pass interference penalty gave Yale a first down on the Southern Bulldogs' 8-yard line. After some line smashes, Curtin turned back to the pass, finding Kelley and firing toward him. But Bond, already making an impact with his kicking, leapt high in front of Kelley and fell in the end zone cradling the ball for a drive-killing interception. The first half ended, 7-7, with no other sustained marches.

Georgia and Yale traded punts to start the second half before Georgia ended up with the ball in good position at Yale's 39. The Southern Bulldogs needed a jolt and brought in reserve halfback Joseph "Cy" Grant, a college baseball star and future minor leaguer who had been battling injuries during football season.

The move worked. After all-SEC fullback George Chapman picked up 11 hard-earned yards on two carries, the shifty Grant ripped off an 18-yard run from the left side. Yale's defense stood tall at the 10-yard line. Georgia needed all four downs before Chapman finally blasted over right tackle for a short touchdown, with Grant kicking successfully for a 14-7 lead.

From there, Georgia's defense suffocated Yale, prohibiting the Elis from crossing midfield while Bond's punting kept Yale pinned against its goal line. Naturally, Yale never relented. The Northern Bulldogs continued to claw out yards and attempt passes for a comeback, and their defense kept Georgia in check.

In the fourth quarter, Yale gained some momentum on offense. Fullback Mather Whitehead caught a short pass and picked up a solid chunk of yards on a run to position the Bulldogs at their own 41.

The next play, a lateral, was designed to go for a big gain as in the first half. Tommy Curtin completed it to halfback Bernard Rankin, who turned upfield with urgency. But he never secured the ball. It popped out on the run and end Henry Wagnon grabbed the ball for Georgia. That play squelched Yale's drive and ended the last significant threat the Bulldogs generated on the afternoon.

In this hard-nosed battle, Georgia rushed for 201 yards and completed one pass. Yale rushed for 118 yards and passed for 48, but their turnovers were ill-timed and costly. When the gun cracked the chilly autumn air as time expired, Georgia's contingent of fans tossed their heavy blankets aside and rushed the field. At dusk, Yale Bowl's goal posts had been torn apart for spoils.

Southern Bulldog, Northern Bulldog

# YALE

## STARTING LINEUP

| | |
|---|---|
| Head Coach: | Raymond Pond |
| Ends: | Robert Train and Lawrence Kelley |
| Tackles: | Meredith Scott and Henry Wright, Jr. |
| Guards: | Francis Curtin (Captain) and Paul Grosscup |
| Center: | James DeAngelis |
| Quarterback: | Thomas Curtin, Jr. |
| Halfbacks: | Bernard Rankin and Stratford Morton |
| Fullback: | Stanley Fuller |

## SUBSTITUTES

| | |
|---|---|
| Guard: | Horace Davis II |
| Fullback: | Mather Whitehead |
| End: | John Overall, Jr. |
| Tackle: | Charles Strauss |
| Halfback: | Richard Cummins |

November 10, 1934

# GEORGIA

### STARTING LINEUP

| | |
|---|---|
| Head Coach: | Harry Mehre |
| Ends: | Charlie Turbyville (Captain) and Henry Wagnon |
| Tackles: | Allen Shi and John West |
| Guards: | Frank Johnson and John Brown |
| Center: | John McKnight |
| Quarterback: | Byron Griffith, Jr. |
| Halfbacks: | John Bond and Al Minot |
| Fullback: | George Chapman |

### SUBSTITUTES

| | |
|---|---|
| Fullback: | John Jones |
| Halfback: | Joseph Grant |
| Tackle: | Charles Opper |
| Quarterback: | Charlie Treadway |
| End: | Alex Ashford |

## Southern Bulldog, Northern Bulldog

Head Coach Pond rallied the Bulldogs after the loss to Georgia and accomplished what his predecessor Root could not. In consecutive weekends, Yale powered over Princeton in New Jersey (7-0) and Harvard in Yale Bowl (14-0) to lord over the Big Three and cap a 5-3 season that brought prestige back to Yale football. The win over Fritz Crisler's Princeton Tigers, a juggernaut and defending co-national champions, still stands as one of the greatest in Yale's history. The Elis snapped Princeton's 15-game winning streak in front of 53,000 fans at Palmer Stadium. Sophomore Larry Kelley scored the lone touchdown on a long pass play, marking his arrival to major college football as a 1934 All-American and future Heisman Trophy winner. The 1934 Yale-Princeton game also marked the final time a major college football team played an entire game as one unit without substitutions, a distinction Yale's iron men earned.

Georgia rolled out of New Haven as a team afire. The Bulldogs shut out North Carolina State (27-0), Auburn (18-0) and Georgia Tech (7-0) to cap an impressive 7-3 campaign. Defensively, the Red and Black allowed seven or fewer points in eight games.

An Associated Press story written the same day as the 1934 Georgia-Yale game succinctly wrapped up this rivalry. For 1935, the Southern Bulldogs removed all intersectional games and faced a more demanding SEC schedule: "Georgia's series with Yale ended today. The L.S.U. Tigers replace Yale on next year's card."

The 11-game series ended with Georgia owning five consecutive wins over Yale, more than any team in history against the Elis at the time. Harvard, the ancient rival, had

November 10, 1934

earned four consecutive wins from 1919 to 1922. Georgia ascended from a regional program to a national name during the series' years, and the Bulldogs stamped their mark in the next decade by winning the 1942 national championship as the SEC grew in stature.

Considered the finest quick-kicker in Georgia Bulldog history, John Bond's punting was a tremendous factor in Georgia's 1934 victory.

# EPILOGUE

Even before the teams' final game, there was a philosophical separation between the schools when it came to football. Georgia was a charter member of the SEC, a dominant conference that shifted power to the South in ensuing decades. Saturdays remain magnificent at Sanford Stadium where tens of thousands pack into the "mini Yale Bowl" to cheer their beloved Bulldogs, who have become one of the all-time winningest programs in college football. In Athens, college football is a significant part of the city's and the school's identity.

Yale's plan to treat football as a natural extension of the classroom and overall college experience continued, though the Elis remained relevant and prominent, especially with two of its players among the first three Heisman Trophy award recipients – Larry Kelley and Clint Frank. The first Heisman winner, Jay Berwanger, came from the University of Chicago, a program that matched Yale's cachet. For decades, the

Maroons were considered a powerhouse, much like Yale, and competed in the Big 10 Conference under distinguished coaches such as Amos Alonzo Stagg and Clark Shaughnessy. As college football became an arms race in the 1930s, the University of Chicago no longer kept pace with Big 10 rivals, and alumni bristled as losses piled up. President Robert Maynard Hutchins found the solution in 1939 – he disbanded the program.

"In many colleges, it is possible for a boy to win 12 letters without learning how to write one," Hutchins commented in The Saturday Evening Post.

Majestic and venerable Stagg Field soon was demolished to construct two libraries on the site.

Yale took a less drastic route than Chicago, but with the same spirit of perspective. The Bulldogs dropped its independent status and joined the Ivy League, which became an official conference in 1954, with like-minded Eastern institutions it battled every autumn. The Ivy League affiliation meant less travel for intersectional games, which were used to help programs create and enhance a reputation. Yale had never scheduled these games heavily; they rarely left New Haven. But even the thought of multiple intersectional games was distasteful in many Yale circles.

In November 1928, Yale Alumni Weekly opined that intersectional games interfered too much with college classes, and all out-of-town games needed to be played within a reasonable distance of New Haven. "The university is not at all interested in matching its football teams with leaders in other sections of the country for the purpose of seeing which type of game is better. The sport is played for the good of the undergraduates and not the public, however friendly that public may be."

What a starkly different world, measured against the current reality of college football teams that spend a significant portion of the fall semester on the road. While Georgia's annual 12- or 13-game schedules feature multiple national television appearances, high-stakes SEC battles that pundits debate endlessly, and glitzy, big-money bowl games in January, Yale games are televised a few times a year and their most important battles still are against Princeton and Harvard, regardless of record. There is no postseason for Yale; football season ends just before Thanksgiving.

In 2018, it's inconceivable that these schools ever were rivals and that Georgia was considered the underdog. Likely, Georgia and Yale will never meet again on the gridiron, remarkable as that would be for those who appreciate the history of both institutions and their football programs, because too much money is at stake in big-time college football. Each Saturday is a precious commodity.

The appeal of this familial connection between Georgia and Yale is the surprising nature of it. They are worlds apart today on the gridiron. To examine a time when roles and perceptions were reversed is to mark the dramatic shift in how college football is viewed in New Haven, Athens, and on both campuses.

Southern Bulldog, Northern Bulldog

## COLLEGE FOOTBALL HALL OF FAME MEMBERS WHO PARTICIPATED IN THE YALE-GEORGIA RIVALRY

# YALE

Albie Booth
Century Milstead
Mal Stevens (player and coach)
Herbert Sturhahn
T.A.D. Jones (coach)
Bill Mallory
Larry Kelley

# GEORGIA

Catfish Smith
Frank Thomas (coach)
Jim Crowley (coach)

# Epilogue

# SELECTED REFERENCES

Newspapers from New York, Atlanta, Chicago and Washington, D.C., provided a tremendous amount of information used in this book. Hundreds of articles and columns were drawn upon.

"A Bowl Full of Memories: 100 Years of Football at the Yale Bowl" by Rich Marazzi; New York, New York; Sports Publishing, 2014.

"A History of American Higher Education" by John R. Thelin; Baltimore, Maryland; The Johns Hopkins University Press, 2011.

"A Pictorial History of the University of Georgia" by F.N. Boney; Athens, Georgia; The University of Georgia Press, 2000.

"About Them Dawgs!: Georgia Football's Memorable Teams and Players" by Patrick Garbin; Latham, Maryland; The Scarecrow Press, 2008.

"Between the Hedges: 100 Years of Georgia Football" by Loran Smith, Ed.; Atlanta, Georgia; Longstreet Press, 1992.

"Between the Hedges: A Story of Georgia Football" by Jesse Outlar; Huntsville, Alabama; The Strode Publishers, 1974.

"Champion of Sport: The Life of Walter Camp 1859-1925" by Kathleen D. Valenzi and Michael W. Hopps; Charlottesville, Virginia; Howell Press, 1990.

Cicotto, Karl. "Bruce Caldwell" Society for American Baseball Research. The Baseball Biography Project. http://sabr.org/bioproj/person/80ee0141

"Games Colleges Play: Scandal and Reform in Intercollegiate Athletics" by John R. Thelin; Baltimore, Maryland; The Johns Hopkins University Press, 1996.

"King Football: Sport and Spectacle in the Golden Age of Radio and Newsreels, Movies and Magazines, the Weekly & the Daily Press" by Michael Oriard; Chapel Hill, North Carolina; The University of North Carolina Press, 2001.

"The Ghosts of Herty Field: Early Days on a Southern Gridiron" by John F. Stegeman; Athens, Georgia; The University of Georgia Press, 1966.

"Yale Bowl and the Open Trolleys" by John D. Somers; Pittsburgh, Pennsylvania; Dorrance Publishing Company, 1997.

"Yale Football: Images of Sport" by Sam Rubin; Mount Pleasant, South Carolina; Arcadia Publishing, 2006.

Selected References

www.ingramcontent.com/pod-product-compliance
Lightning Source LLC
Chambersburg PA
CBHW031114080526
44587CB00011B/971